ROCK GARDENING

A BLANDFORD
GARDENING HANDBOOK

ROCK
GARDENING

Peter McHoy

BLANDFORD PRESS
POOLE · NEW YORK · SYDNEY

First published in the UK 1986 by Blandford Press,
Link House, West Street, Poole, Dorset, BH15 1LL

Distributed in the United States by
Sterling Publishing Co., Inc.,
2 Park Avenue, New York, N.Y. 10016

Distributed in Australia by
Capricorn Link (Australia) Pty Ltd.
PO Box 665, Lane Cove, NSW 2066

British Library Cataloguing in Publication Data

McHoy, Peter
　Rock gardening.—(A Blandford gardening handbook)
　1. Alpine garden plants
　I. Title
　635.9′672　　　　　　　　SB421

ISBN 0 7137 1575 8 (Hardback)
　　0 7137 1578 2 (Paperback)

All photographs by Peter McHoy
and line drawings by Paula Chasty

Typeset by Megaron Typesetting, Bournemouth, Dorset

Printed in Portugal by Printer Portuguesa

CONTENTS

INTRODUCTION

Anyone who visits an alpine plant show for the first time is likely to be either enraptured by the infinite small-scale beauty of the plants and converted to an alpine enthusiast on the spot, or completely deterred by the bewildering array of names (many of which will be unfamiliar even to an experienced gardener) and the clearly erudite knowledge of the enthusiasts exhibiting. It is easy, as a first impression, to feel that it is part of some exclusive club beyond one's reach.

This book is written with the hope that it might be a small bridge between

A rock garden at the Chelsea show, London, in 1982. Although rocks of this size are difficult to obtain and to work with, it shows what can be achieved even on a relatively small site.

'ordinary' gardening and the fascinating world of 'alpine' gardening.

Alpine gardening is undoubtedly a completely absorbing interest, and it can become a collector's hobby in a way that is not feasible with trees, shrubs or herbaceous border plants. The diminutive size of alpine plants makes it possible to collect different species of plants rather as a philatelist collects stamps. Some even collect particular groups; saxifragas, sedums or sempervivums for instance. Size of garden is no real restriction, for you can easily have a collection of 20 or so alpines in a small trough or planted in a single block of tufa stone.

The days of major rock garden construction on the grand scale have gone. Transport is expensive, manpower even more so, and in any case gardens are generally smaller. Ideas about rock gardens have changed, and smaller rock outcrops are more fashionable than the cliff-type rock features of the past. This book reflects that, and there is plenty of advice on how to get the best from a relatively small area.

You do not even need a rock garden at all to grow alpines. The whole of your alpine gardening can be done in troughs and pots (indeed the plants that you see at shows will almost certainly be growing in pots). Quite simply, alpine gardening is for everyone. The aim of this book has been to encourage that belief.

People approach alpine gardening from different viewpoints, of course; for some it is the individual plants that appeal, to others it is the rock garden or alpine trough as a garden feature, and the plants may be a means to that end. Between those extremes lie all shades of opinion. This book is intended to take the beginner from the first steps to a firm foothold into the hobby; it should also act as a useful reference to anyone already interested in alpines who wants a handbook of basic facts at their fingertips.

1·USING ALPINES

The title of this book is *Rock Gardening*. 'Alpine gardening' can have connotations of rare, perhaps tiny and sometimes weedy-looking plants grown by life-long enthusiasts who talk a dialect of gardening that is sometimes hardly comprehensible to the horticulturally less educated. It is an erroneous assumption, of course, for alpines are for everyone.

To describe alpines as 'rock plants' carries its own risks − it implies that you need a rock garden to enjoy them. A rock garden provides a ideal setting for most of them, but there are many more ways of growing alpine plants. The keen exhibitor will grow his best plants in pots; and many keen enthusiasts have a greenhouse and frames devoted to alpines. Then there are gravel gardens, dry stone walls, raised beds and sink gardens, all of which will make a good home and setting for these plants. Rocks are *not* a prerequisite for gardening with alpines. For that reason the term 'alpine' has generally been used throughout this book when referring to the plants.

It is possible to plant alpines in all kinds of odd spots, such as among the cracks or holes in paving. This plant is *Armeria maritima*

GARDENING WITH ALPINES

It is important to be clear what you want from your alpine gardening. If your imagination has been caught by some of the magnificent rock gardens on the grand scale, and you have a suitable site on which to construct perhaps a smaller version yourself, it is inevitable that this, as much as the beauty of individual alpine plants, is going to be your prime interest.

Aspirations to a 'proper' rock garden should never be discouraged, and there are detailed instructions on how to build one in Chapter 2. Rocks are expensive, however, and it *is* difficult to create a

natural-looking rock garden in a modern suburban garden, and if your interest lies in the plants themselves then there is no reason why you should not be equally happy with one of the alternatives.

Although a large rock garden on a sunny sloping site is the dream of many, you can make a worthwhile miniature alpine garden in something as tiny as an old sink. No other group of plants is so easily accommodated whatever the size or scope of the garden. You can have a respectable collection of alpines in a garden where it would be impossible to

Stone sinks are popular for alpines. Natural stone sinks are now rare and expensive, but artificial troughs are a good substitute. You can make these yourself (see page 40 – 1).

have more than say a couple of large shrubs or small trees. If you have room for a greenhouse and a garden frame, then you have the scope for a collection of alpines in pots that will provide year-round interest.

The worst situation is attempting to create a natural rock feature in a setting that is clearly wrong. The chances are

9

In a really intensively planted rock garden the rocks serve mainly as punctuation points. A mixed planting like this, though very attractive, needs a lot of maintenance.

The rock plants in this low bank are all vigorous types, but they are extremely colourful in flower and you need bold plants in a position like this.

that it will look either pretentious or ridiculous.

THE OPTIONS

Inevitably any list of suggestions has to start with a rock feature. Well done, and in the right setting, a rock garden looks superb. It *is* possible to create quite a dramatic and realistic-looking rock feature even in a small corner of the garden (see the picture on page 11), but it needs considerable skill and a very careful selection of suitable rocks to bring this off. It is much better to have a rock garden in an open position, ideally in a sunny aspect on sloping ground.

An ideal is one thing, reality another. If the garden is otherwise suitable, and you are really determined, you could possibly create a slight slope by earth-moving efforts. More practically, it is worth going in for rock outcrops; island beds with rocks that look as though they have surfaced through the surrounding soil. These can be quite economical of rock and are far less likely to look incongruous on a small scale or in the setting of a modern garden.

A scree is another possibility, and for this you will need comparatively few rocks, but these are rather specialist features and best in association with a rock garden anyway. You could, however, adapt the idea and have a gravelled area with a few rocks set within it. As the picture on page 10 shows, although clearly artificial in approach this can look attractive even in a small area.

The other alternatives make no pretence at reproducing nature. They simply let the plants speak for themselves.

Raised beds are well worth considering. They will bring the plants that much nearer to eye level so that you can appreciate them more readily, and provided that you do not mortar the blocks

A small bed using tufa rock. The owner has managed to pack lots of interesting plants into a relatively small area.

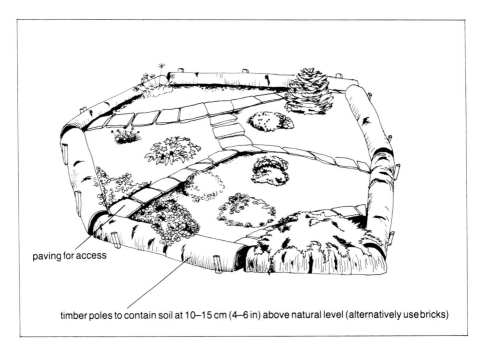

paving for access

timber poles to contain soil at 10–15 cm (4–6 in) above natural level (alternatively use bricks)

There are many alternatives if you lack space or a suitable site for a rock garden. This walk-about low raised bed is one possibility.

or stones the sides provide additional planting space for many worthwhile alpines.

If all you have is a tiny paved garden it is still possible to enjoy alpines in pots, especially if you have room for a greenhouse and frames. Even if you have a large garden you may eventually want to try this form of alpine gardening. It gives you a much better opportunity to enjoy the plants at close quarters, lets you get to know the plants and their requirements more easily, and will enable you to grow some of the more challenging plants

that might be difficult in the open garden.

A flat site can lend itself to a 'walk-about' bed of generous proportions (it needs to be fairly large to be effective). The area becomes a large island bed with stepping-stone pathways (*natural* stone please!) through the bed to give access to the plants for maintenance and to make it possible to walk among the plants to enjoy them. A bed like this can be set into a large lawn with just a depression at the edge to make it possible to mow and trim a clean edge. Or you could raise the bed slightly, using a formal edging such as natural stone or an informal edge such as thick rustic poles (stripped of bark). The latter, although giving a nice appearance

Although not as natural-looking as a rock outcrop, in the right setting a small island rock bed will give plenty of scope for growing a wide range of alpines.

to the bed, can make it difficult to set within a lawn.

There are other ways in which you can squeeze in a few more alpines; quite a few will grow happily among paving or at the edge of a path.

Finally, do not overlook alpines as general garden plants. Some, such as *Acaena microphylla*, can make general ground-cover plants, and armerias and dianthus make pretty edging plants for a border, whereas plants such as *Dianthus deltoides*, aubrieta, and *Alyssum saxatile*

In a small garden a simple rock outcrop may be all you can find space for, but it can be impressive nevertheless.

13

Rock and water associate well, and where you have space it is worth trying to combine the two.

would not look amiss at the front of a herbaceous border.

WHAT IS AN ALPINE?

The term alpine has been used freely throughout this book; and it is used a lot in garden centres and by gardeners; but the term can mean different things to different people, so it is worth being clear about our definitions.

Firstly, alpines are not necessarily plants that come from the Alps. To a botanist the term suggests plants that in nature grow above the tree line (the height to which trees grow) but below the

permanent snow line. To a gardener the term is likely to mean any low, dwarf or slow-growing plant that can effectively be used in the rock garden. That may include some plants that are not really mountain plants at all.

A more subtle distinction is occasionally made by gardeners: there is sometimes a tendency to speak of the choicer, non-invasive, generally dainty plants as

This narrow bed between drive and boundary has been made into a kind of scree bed. The bed also contains plenty of bulbs to flower in winter or early spring, to maintain interest during the bleaker months.

'alpines', and the coarser more rampant plants such as aubrieta and snow in summer *(Cerastium tomentosum)* as 'rock plants'. This is little more than horti-cultural snobbery, and is not used here.

This chapter cannot give you a blueprint for building a rock garden stone by stone; every site, every rock, is different. Even professionals accustomed to constructing the sort of rock garden features seen in display gardens decide on the exact placing of the rocks only on site with the rocks before them. Perhaps more than any other form of garden construction, making a rock garden is as much artistry as muscle-power.

In the days of the great rock garden displays at the Chelsea Flower Show in London, which were world famous, some of the designers have been described standing in front of their team of men like a conductor using his 'orchestra' to get the very best from the rocks; with a little lift there, a slight shift here, and a change of emphasis somewhere else.

That does not mean that the whole process should be surrounded with mystique. There are basic principles that are straightforward, and which should give very satisfactory results.

THE RIGHT SITE

A few alpines will grow well in shade. The vast majority need the sunniest position possible. Even a rock garden in a sunny position will have a few shady spots in which you can grow those plants that tolerate poor light, but the more open and the sunnier the site the better.

Some compromise may be necessary, but never make a rock garden beneath the shade of trees. Not only will the shade cause its own problems, but the soil will also probably be very dry and falling leaves will cause endless problems for low-growing plants that may almost be buried beneath them. Slugs and snails, and fungus diseases, will also take a heavy toll. As a general rule, alpines do not like damp winters, and drips from a tree will finish off many of them.

Having said that, it may be that a screen of trees or shrubs will create a suitable background for a rock garden if it hides an even more artificial outlook, such as a fence or a brick wall. The screen must, of course, be far enough away not to cause shade problems.

If there are no natural slopes it may be possible to excavate some of the ground in front of the rock garden to lower the paths and surrounding ground, using the excavated soil to increase the height of the actual rock bed. This is a very labour-intensive job, especially as it is necessary to keep subsoil at subsoil level, and the topsoil on top. It may be necessary to

16

This is a famous rock garden – the limestone rock outcrop at the Cambridge Botanic Garden, England.

remove the topsoil from the rock area, use the excavated soil from the surrounding area to build up height, then return the topsoil. By that time you may be wondering whether one of the alternatives might not have been a better idea.

If the water table is low, and the fall of the land right, a sunken rock garden is a distinct possibility. It may also provide an opportunity to combine the rock

garden with a 'stream' and pool in a natural way. Excavating to any depth will inevitably mean much hard work (and could well involve a pick-axe as well as a spade), and you will have to provide a layer of suitable soil for the plants to grow in. It is not an easy option, but worth considering if the garden lends itself to this treatment.

A partially shady slope does have possibilities. It will grow a wide range of plants that prefer cooler conditions. Many ericaceous and other acid-loving plants are likely to thrive if the soil is not alkaline. Autumn gentians, dwarf ferns, and many of the primulas should be quite happy.

It may be possible to create a bank by buying in topsoil, so avoiding some of the excavation necessary to create a bank, but if you have to barrow the soil yourself this will still not be an easy option.

Although rock gardens are often associated with quite steep slopes, perhaps where other forms of gardening would be

Right: A 'currants in a bun' type of rock garden that nowadays you are always advised not to construct. Yet this is an historic rock garden, perhaps the oldest in the world, constructed in 1772 in the Chelsea Physic Garden, London, from rock brought back from Iceland.

A rock garden on the grand scale, at Alton Towers, Staffordshire, England.

difficult, a rock outcrop is an excellent way to break up a large, open lawn. If the lawn is big enough, a whole series of rock outcrops will look quite natural and provide plenty of scope for growing a wide range of alpines. Rock outcrops, with just the tips of the rock appearing through the soil on a gentle slope, give the impression of there being much more rock than there is in reality. By choosing suitable, relatively small, pieces you can give the impression that there is a lot more beneath the surface. This is a consideration if cost is a restraint.

DRAINAGE

Anyone who has had to dig a soakaway and lay land drains will know that it is a job to be avoided if at all possible. Nevertheless alpines generally need well-drained soil, and if the ground is prone to waterlogging some attempts at drainage

Rock garden construction is heavy work to start with, so you do not want to make needless chores. But if the ground is badly drained, whether you are constructing a rock garden or a scree, it may be necessary to lay land drains.

are essential. Unless the soil is already free-draining, excavate at least the top 30 cm (1 ft) of soil, and fill the bottom 15 cm (6 in) with hardcore, small stones, or gravel. If drainage is really poor, you will need to run land drains to a convenient point that will take surplus water away from the rock garden; generally, however, this is unnecessary. Cover the hardcore or gravel with inverted turves if possible, but unless you have cut the bed out of a lawn this may be a problem. Otherwise top with fine gravel or pea shingle before returning the soil.

SOIL OR COMPOST

Normal garden soil may sometimes be perfectly adequate for alpines, but it will almost always be worth improving it. If the soil if very clayey it may be best to buy in better topsoil.

You have only one chance to get the soil right, as you will hardly want to keep rebuilding your rock garden. It is well worth mixing 3 parts of soil (buy in topsoil if your own is really poor), 2 parts of moss peat, and 1½ parts of sharp sand or grit. Add 3 kg of bonemeal to every cubic metre of this mix (5 lb to every cubic yard). Make sure all the ingredients are mixed thoroughly.

THE ROCKS

Finding suitable rockery stone is almost as difficult as positioning it. Unless you have a very generous budget, rocks such as the highly desirable weatherworn limestones are likely to be prohibitively expensive. If you live in an area where such stone is found then it is an obvious choice because it will blend in with the landscape and you will not have the substantial carriage costs that make such stone so expensive in more distant parts.

As a rule it is best to use stones from the region in which you live. They are likely to be cheaper and will generally blend in more readily with the surroundings. If you live in an area where there are no local stones, then you will probably find your local merchant has a wide selection of stones from quite far afield, but of course you will pay a premium for this.

If you need a lot of stone, say about 10 tonnes or more, it may be worth contacting quarries direct even if they are some distance away, to see whether they will deliver a load direct. This may work out cheaper than using a stone merchant or going to a garden centre. If you live reasonably near a quarry it is always worth contacting them anyway to see what they can offer. Even some sand pits may have sandstone for sale.

Try to choose your own rocks if possible. Most stone merchants and garden centres should let you do this; they may give you a pallet to put them on, and weigh them afterwards. Others may be less precise, glance over your heap of rocks, and quote you a price. Buying rockery stone is not the precise business that buying say building blocks can be.

If you do select your own rocks you will soon find that there has to be a compromise between those large pieces that look really good and what you can actually manage to lift or move. Try to include plenty of large rocks, but do not go in for pieces that you cannot handle.

Knowing how much rock you need is by no means easy – a heap that seems reasonably generous can seem depressingly inadequate once you start to build the rock garden – especially as much of the rock will be hidden from view once it is in position.

As a guide, a tonne of sandstone might contain perhaps 30 pieces, with large individual rocks weighing more than 50 kg (1 cwt). To relate size to weight, imagine a 50 kg (1 cwt) bag of cement; a rock of similar weight will be about as big as that.

Unfortunately rock is sometimes sold by weight, sometimes by the cubic metre or yard. As an approximate guide, a cubic metre/yard of sandstone might be enough for 4 m^2 (5 sq yd) of rockery; two tonnes might be enough for a 9 m^2 (11 sq yd) rock garden on a gentle slope, but for a cliff effect on a steep slope you could easily use another tonne. These are very broad generalisations, and it is best to check with your supplier, telling him the area that you want to cover.

If just a few rocks are required to add interest to a scree or for a small island bed they can be bought as individual rocks and costed in 50 kg (1 cwt) units.

It is better to buy a few large rocks than a lot of small ones (too many small ones

Some stones that look rather stark when new will look attractive once they have weathered.

of about the same size often looks monotonous and boring).

The amount of compost needed can be surprising too. It is best to allow 0.75 m^3 (1 cu yd) of compost for every tonne of rock; more of course if you plan to build it into an artificial slope.

Although the type of rock available will depend on the part of the world in which you live, the characteristics of the following rocks represent most of those that you are likely to encounter.

Limestone Limestones are formed from the shell remains of minute sea creatures, and have a high lime content, although chalk itself is too soft for using as a rock. Generally limestones are whitish, light-cream, grey, bluish, or buff-coloured, depending on the area from which they are quarried. Different

A carboniferous limestone.

A sandstone.

limestones also have different characteristics: some are easily split into thin flagstones, for instance; others are not. Limestone can look harsh when newly-quarried. It is rugged with strong strata marks, but if the rock is of the 'soft' type it may be damaged by frost. It is good for making cliffs, banks, and terraces.

Weathered limestone has a creamy-white to dark grey colour, and because it is weathered will be moss or lichen-covered. However, in an industrial atmosphere, or near the sea, it tends to lose this covering and become bleached to a dirty white. It has clear strata marks. This kind of stone is not suitable for walls or paving, but is superb for a fairly flat rock garden and in association with water, perhaps edging a pool or stream.

Sandstone A dark brown stone sometimes tinged purplish or greenish, sand-

stone lacks strata marks. It tends to be rather angular and best for a bold rock outcrop. *Gritstone* (sometimes called millstone grit) is a very coarse sandstone. It is a hard, generally buff-coloured stone with no strata markings. Quarried pieces can be rather angular, but it weathers attractively.

Tufa This pumice-like rock is a form of limestone. It is a brash, buff-coloured rock, almost dazzlingly white in sunlight when newly quarried, but within months it mellows to grey. This unusual rock, which is porous and full of tiny holes, and soft enough to drill easily to make planting holes, is seldom used for a large-scale rock garden. It is, however, ideally suited for sink gardens, raised beds, window-boxes, or even as a free-standing rock as a decorative feature planted with alpines (see page 47). Tufa is a very light

23

rock, but it becomes much heavier when it is wet, so if buying by weight buy in a dry period!

Granite is an extremely hard volcanic rock, reddish, purple-brown, green or blue-grey. It is rather acid and useful for lime-hating plants. The pieces are often angular and weather very slowly.

Slate is not a common choice, but it can look very effective used with a water course (see illustration on page 14). Colours include green, blue-grey, or purplish. The pieces are rather angular when quarried, and the surfaces rather flat, but the rock weathers well.

Artificial rock It is possible to buy boulders made from hollow moulded concrete. These sound off-putting, but are finished in a grey or sandy colour and have a rough, gritty surface, and above all they look impressive. The pieces are certainly lighter than conventional rock, but they are by no means cheaper. Weight for weight it can be very much more expensive than the best natural stone, but of course being hollow you can actually have a bigger rockery from the same weight of stone.

It is even possible to buy glass-fibre (glass- reinforced plastic) rocks that are very light and surprisingly realistic.

PREPARING THE GROUND

Good ground preparation makes sound sense for most gardening jobs, but nowhere is it more important than for the rock garden. Anyone who has tried to weed a rockery over-run with ground elder or couch grass (now not the problem that it was; see page 116) will know the importance of clearing the ground of perennial weeds before you start.

In an ideal world you would clear the ground twelve months beforehand and continually work to remove all traces of difficult perennial weeds, and to reduce drastically the population of annuals. Few of us are that patient, but it is a good idea to prepare the ground in summer, construct the rock garden in autumn, and plant in spring. This will give you a fair chance to clear the ground of most weeds. If you are impatient to make a start with the plants, you could plant a few shrubs and dwarf conifers in autumn, together with some pockets of spring-flowering bulbs to bring some early colour, but wait until spring for the main planting.

Always prepare an area of ground bigger than the outcrop or rock garden, in case you change the design as you build. Contour the land as much as possible before you start to lay the rocks. Leave plenty of compost for filling in afterwards.

LAYING THE ROCKS

Do *not* have the rocks dumped where you are actually going to build; otherwise they will have to be moved twice. Try to have them as close as possible, however. Lay the rocks out so that you can inspect them.

An outcrop The first stone (the *key stone*) is the most important one, and it will largely dictate how the rest look. So make it a large one, and preferably with an interesting shape. There is no magic about starting at the top or the bottom – either will do.

Make the hole larger than the rock, so that it is easy to manoeuvre, but it should

Rock outcrops can be very successful and are well worth considering if you lack a suitable site for a traditional rock garden. They do not need a large amount of rock and can be made to look very natural within a large lawn.

not be so deep that too much of the rock is buried. Although a good portion of the rock should be beneath the soil, it is wasteful of rock to bury it needlessly deep; it is the level and position of the rocks above ground that should dictate the exact depth. They should, of course, look as though they continue into the soil and not appear to sit on the surface.

The top should run slightly downwards towards the back and into any slope. Any strata lines should be horizontal on the face. Not all rocks have strata lines of course, so this may not be possible.

It may take some time to get the key stone right; be prepared to move it a number of times, even if this means

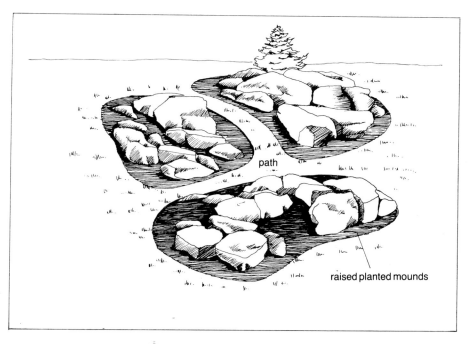

path

raised planted mounds

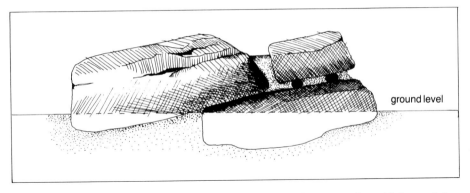

ground level

Try to place the rocks so that there are plenty of planting pockets and crevices.

redigging the hole. Look at it from various angles before being satisfied.

Once the key stone is in the right position, firm the soil all around it by ramming it with a piece of wood to remove any air pockets that could make the rock unstable or cause the roots to dry out.

Add more rocks, working outwards from the key stone, always matching

strata on the same plane if the rock has strata marks. Colour is important too; try to match shades as closely as possible, so that each rock looks as though it belongs in juxtaposition with the others.

There is no need to pack the rocks closely together, but if you do not have enough large stones it may be possible to group two or three close together so that they look as though they are part of one large rock.

Most rock outcrops are likely to be on fairly shallow slopes, but if you are making one on a steep slope the rocks on the upper layers should rest on the lower rocks. Avoid a building-block effect; it is more natural to have fissures running vertically through each layer.

Fill the pockets between the rocks with compost, ramming it beneath the rocks to ensure stability. The soil in the pockets will probably settle, so be prepared to top them up a week or two later.

Soil being packed round a simple sandstone rock outcrop. It is important to make sure there are no air pockets beneath the rocks.

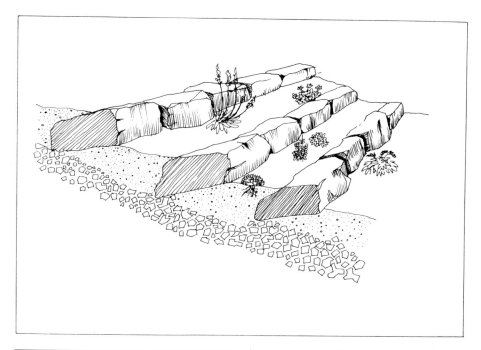

'CLIFF-BUILDING'

On a naturally sloping site, a more traditional rock garden reflecting the grand style of a previous generation could be tried, though modified to suit the modern garden. Much of the advice for rock outcrops obviously applies to this form of rock garden too. This time, however, the rocks are arranged in tiers down the slope. This is where large rocks really come into their own.

Sloping the rocks back slightly where they meet the earth will carry the rainwater into the ground where it is of more use to the plants. For a natural effect, embed the back edge of the rocks into the earth and leave the front face exposed. This will give the rock garden a more cliff-like appearance.

Again lay the largest and most attractive stone first. With these large stones, make sure the subsoil is rammed firm, and if necessary ram hardcore into any depression that may cause the rock to sink. Obviously this is only likely to be necessary with very heavy rocks.

Decide where you are going to position the other major stones, then arrange the smaller ones between them. It is worth

27

28

Moving rocks is heavy work, and carelessness can easily cause injury. These illustrations show some techniques for moving rocks. Whenever possible, get someone strong to help you.

setting some rocks a little forward or back a bit from the main face of the 'cliff' so that it does not look too wall-like.

MOVING ROCKS

Building a rock garden is heavy work. Trying to lift heavy rocks may cause serious injury, so do not try to treat rock garden building as a weight-lifting exercise. There is no need to lift and carry rocks. Use the principle of leverage wherever possible.

One of the most useful aids is a *strong* sack trolley. You will need plenty of strong planks to move the trolley over grass and soft earth. You may be able to borrow or hire a sack trolley. If not consider rolling the rocks along a strong board supported on rollers (iron pipes, or even old broom handles will do), moving the back rollers to the front as you proceed.

Do not try to make do with a wheelbarrow; it will not be made for this sort of work, and you will in any case still be involved in lifting the rocks into the barrow (clearly not a good idea).

Slopes pose particular problems. If the slope is steep you may have to depend on a long, strong plank, rope, and plenty of help. Even quite large pieces can be pulled up a slope with the concerted effort of helpers pulling on a rope securely tied around the rock while others push it up the plank from below. The most important advice is not to rush the job. Taking your time will probably make the job easier, and certainly safer.

Once the rock is approximately in position, manoeuvre it by levering with a crowbar. You can actually move rocks quite a long way by this method, rolling them end over end. Only work with rocks in dry, frost-free weather. Wet earth is not only unpleasant to work with, it is also slippery and therefore dangerous.

3·RAISED BEDS

A raised bed is unlikely to be a cheap option. Material for the walls will probably cost you just as much as rocks for a rock bed, and you may be faced with the additional cost of soil and other compost materials to fill the raised beds.

Raised beds may lack any financial incentive, but they have other attractions. Sometimes a rock outcrop or traditional rock garden quite simply will not fit into the overall design of the garden. You may just want the charm of the inevitably small alpine plants to be that much nearer eye level. You will also find the plants that much easier to tend, and the weeds that little bit easier to cope with.

If plants are your main interest, a raised bed is all that you need, and if the walls are built of suitable material you have plenty of scope for planting in the walls too.

From the point of view of the plants the exact size and shape is not particularly important. The main considerations have to be how the beds fit into the overall garden design, and how practical they are for access; anything over 60 cm (2 ft) wide is likely to make cultivation difficult in a one-sided bed, up to 1.2 m (4 ft) is perfectly acceptable for an island bed that can be reached from all sides.

It is worth considering a raised bed for alpines to replace a narrow border, perhaps between path and boundary, that is really inadequate for most herbaceous plants and shrubs. Clearly you will not be able to pile soil up against a boundary fence, but it may be possible to build a wall using releatively cheap building blocks, leaving a gap between fence and raised bed. Do, however, consider the problems of maintaining or replacing the fence in years to come.

There is less of a problem if the boundary is already a wall, but it is worth painting the wall with a waterproof paint (a garden centre may sell these for ponds; otherwise consult a builder's merchant). Never build a raised bed using a wall of your home as the back; you will bridge the damp-proof course. Raised beds do not have to be high to be effective. Generally 60 cm (2 ft) is adequate.

MATERIALS

Solid concrete, concrete blocks and bricks all have a harsh appearance that is far from ideal for a raised alpine bed. If you must use these, old bricks or those with a 'rustic' finish will probably look much better than a new facing brick.

Concrete blocks can sometimes be improved with a cement paint in a subdued colour. Bricks or blocks that have to be mortared together also reduce the opportunities for planting in the crevices. You can leave sections of mortar out for planting, but this seldom looks as satisfactory as a dry stone wall.

Dry stone walling is often regarded as a craft rather than a normal garden construction job, but in fact there is nothing particularly complicated about erecting a wall about 60 cm (2 ft) high, and the basic techniques are described below.

Dry stone walls are sometimes used simply as dividing walls, and it is possible to grow a few suitable plants in these. Consider first the possibility of making the wall with a small cavity that you can fill with soil. This will provide plenty of planting scope for alpines, and should make a much more attractive feature of the wall.

BUILDING A DRY STONE WALL

The starting point is to phone round your local quarries, if there are any, or consult a few stone merchants. This will

A dry stone wall constructed from slate. Although rather stark and angular, it is possible to grow plants with slate.

A random stone wall like this, using a more mellow rock, is a good choice if you want to grow a range of plants in the crevices.

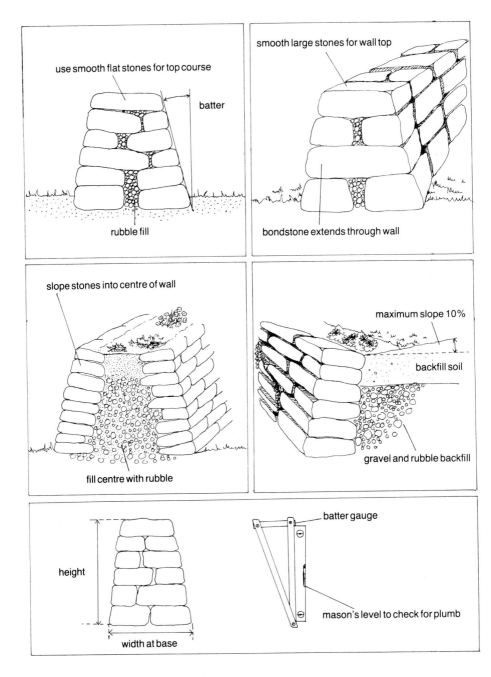

use smooth flat stones for top course

batter

rubble fill

smooth large stones for wall top

bondstone extends through wall

slope stones into centre of wall

fill centre with rubble

maximum slope 10%

backfill soil

gravel and rubble backfill

height

width at base

batter gauge

mason's level to check for plumb

Dry stone walls provide plenty of planting opportunities in the crevices. There are many types of dry stone walling, but these illustrations show the principles involved.

not only give you an indication of prices, but will give you a good idea of what suitable stone is available. As with stone for a rock garden, so much depends on where you live, and what is available from local sources, that generalisations are difficult. Be sure to explain that you want the stone for walling.

Making a start Even if you are keeping the wall low (say 60 cm/2 ft), it is

worth laying a foundation, and this is especially necessary on soil that might be unstable. A shallow trench filled with compacted hardcore and earth may provide a base that is solid enough, but it is usually worth laying a concrete foundation. The general rule is to make the footing (wall foundation) twice as wide as the width of the wall, with the blocks or stones laid in the centre. As walling stone does not come in standard measurements, you will obviously have to use some

If you lack a suitable site for a rock bed in a natural setting, there is a lot to be said for creating a rock outcrop in a raised bed like this.

discretion. Whatever type of material you use for the walls, the first course should start a couple of inches below soil level, for added stability.

Gravity and careful positioning of the stones dictate the strength of a dry stone wall. The illustration on page 32 shows the principles involved in dry wall construction. Make sure there are plenty of large stones in the lower portion of the wall, and use most of the smaller stones near the top. If the wall is more than 60 cm (2 ft) high, or if it is a retaining wall, there should also be a batter (slope), so that the top of the wall slopes in at about 1 in 12.

Place the large *bondstones* at each end of the wall and at intervals along the footing. These should extend through the entire width of the wall to give stability.

Complete the first course of stones by laying them in position between the bondstones. Use large stones in the first course and near the base of the wall. In the vast majority of stone walls, the stones are laid flat side down. There are a few regional techniques that use stones on edge, but this calls for more skill and if this is your first drystone wall it is wise to keep it simple. It will be necessary to adjust the position and perhaps change some stones to avoid large gaps in the first course.

Start the next course by placing several stones at one end, making sure they fit together with no movement. Place more stones across the width of the wall and slope others towards the centre; tilting the stones inwards slightly forces the

weight of the stones to rest against each other and so help stability. It also helps to ensure a slight narrowing towards the top of the wall. Use small stones to fill in the gaps in the middle of the wall and between larger stones.

Bear in mind the need for the batter (slope) for free-standing walls above 60 cm (2 ft) and on retaining walls, and use a batter gauge if necessary (see illustration on page 32). Use flat, broad stones for the top course, so that they serve rather like coping stones. Place soil between the courses, not only because it is useful for the plants but also to act as a crude form of mortar.

Coursed and random walls Purely random patterns can look fine for a retaining wall, in say a terraced garden, but for a more formal raised bed coursed walls generally look more acceptable. You will, of course, need to use more regular stones for this, and you should seek the advice of your stone merchant. Dressed (cut) stone of fairly even thickness will be easier to work with.

ALTERNATIVES TO STONE

Stone is a natural choice for raised beds for alpines, but it is not heresy to use bricks or concrete walling blocks; you simply lose the opportunity to plant in the sides, and unless the walls are low or the bed wide you may end up with a lot of conspicuous wall in relation to the plants. Try to keep walls of this type low

and make sure there are plenty of trailing plants at the edge to soften the appearance.

Railway sleepers (railroad ties) can make quite attractive raised beds for alpines; although planting in the sides is not really practical they have a natural appearance that does not look amiss. If you have a local supply of railway sleepers, this kind of bed is well worth

Plants such as campanulas will seed themselves freely and soon become established in the crevices of a retaining wall like this.

considering in a suitable setting. They are heavy to manhandle of course, and you need plenty of help.

Even breeze-blocks should not be discounted if they are available cheaply, and the plants are more important than the

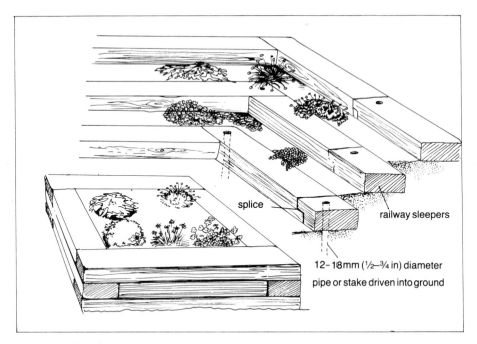

splice

railway sleepers

12-18mm (½-¾ in) diameter
pipe or stake driven into ground

bed as a feature in its own right. For anyone who finds bending difficult but gets immense pleasure from the delights of alpines, raised beds of any of these materials could expand the hobby considerably.

Some examples of raised beds made from railway sleepers and other materials are illustrated below. All can be acceptable; but whether they are right in a particular instance depends on the setting for them.

Old wooden railway sleepers (railroad ties) are heavy to work with, but they make strong, long-lasting, and surprisingly attractive, raised beds. They are well worth considering if you have a local and inexpensive supply. This illustration shows two of the many ways in which they can be used.

and more open the site the better. Good drainage is still important, though in a raised bed made from dry stone walling there will be enough drainage from the sides, so nothing more need be done if you use a free-draining compost such as the one described on page 56.

Beds with solid walls, such as brick or mortared blocks, may still become water-

SITE AND SOIL

The same criteria apply to raised beds as to rock gardens; generally, the sunnier

Iberis sempervirens, at home on a wall.

Aubrieta, another splendid wall plant.

logged at times if the ground beneath is compacted and poorly drained. If it is a heavy, sticky clay it may be worth excavating 45 cm (18 in) of it and filling this with hardcore or gravel.

You do not need to fill the whole bed with good compost. The bottom half can be taken up with something with free drainage like gravel and stone or brick rubble. This will have to be topped with inverted turves or something like gravel

and pea shingle before topping with the soil mix described on page 56.

Be particularly careful if you have to buy in soil to fill the beds. Try to see what you are buying; and be prepared to wait before planting so that you can see whether you have imported a weed problem.

The soil in a raised bed will almost certainly settle after a week or two. It is better to wait until it settles, then top it up before planting. Topping up is much more difficult once the bed has been planted.

4·SINKS, TROUGHS AND TUFA

There is nothing inferior about growing your alpines in sinks and troughs. It does not make you a second-rate alpine enthusiast. Nor does it mean that the range of plants that you grow need be severely limited. If you choose the right plants it is quite feasible to grow 50 plants in a sink or trough measuring only 90×60 cm (3×2 ft), without them being overcrowded, so with half a dozen containers like this you could grow hundreds of plants.

For anyone with a tiny garden, or with a setting that simply does not lend itself to natural rock landscaping, sinks and troughs provide an ideal solution.

A trough garden in an old stone sink.

TRADITIONAL STONE SINKS

Interest in sink gardening began when old stone sinks were being replaced with the then modern glazed sinks. They could be bought cheaply; often they were yours for the trouble of taking them away.

Nowadays genuine stone sinks and troughs are difficult to obtain, and expensive when you find them. For just an isolated trough as a garden feature you may feel that the genuine article is a worthwhile investment. If you need a number of them, some of the alternatives will probably be a better proposition.

There are reconstituted stone sinks or troughs. These are not cheap, but they usually have the merit of being of better proportions than real stone sinks, which are sometimes rather shallow.

Glazed sinks are often available for the cost of taking them away, but they are hardly elegant and need to be converted into something more attactive. Step-by-step instructions for coating a glazed sink with 'hypertufa' are given on page 42, but bear in mind that these sinks are very heavy even before you add a layer of concrete. They are certainly not to be moved with compost in them too. Sinks of this type are best supported off the ground on bricks, then prepared on site.

If you are going to make a hypertufa mix there is much to be said for making the whole trough from scratch. The proportions will certainly be more acceptable than those of converted glazed sinks, which tend to look deep and rather square. Details of how to make your own hypertufa sink appear on page 41.

Any of the sinks based on concrete will weather in time but can look rather stark initially. The appearance can be im-

If converting a glazed sink, make sure the glazed area that will take the adhesive is clean. Use a wire brush and a detergent to remove grease.

Once the sink is clean, brush on a PVA adhesive.

40

Slap on the hypertufa mix (see text), using protective gloves.

Mould the hypertufa over the rim and take it down to just below compost level.

proved by painting the surface with something that will encourage algae, moss and lichen to grow. There are many recipes, most of the traditional ones being based on things like cow manure. These are hardly practical for the vast majority of people, and you may have to make do with a solution of an ordinary liquid fertiliser. Another alternative is to paint the surface occasionally with water used for boiling rice. It provides a slightly glutinous surface on which moss and lichen spores find an easy home. Any of these should speed up the weathering process, so you can take your pick.

MAKING A HYPERTUFA TROUGH

1) On a firm, flat surface, make a 2.5 cm (1 in) bed of moist sand, larger than the finished trough. As you will be using bricks or concrete walling blocks for the mould, the size should be a multiple of these. Eight bricks on edge will give you a trough with an inside area of about 45 × 30 cm (18 × 12 in). Lay the bricks in position on the sand and cover them with a sheet of polythene, tucking it in neatly at the edges. Then mould the damp sand to form a smooth curved channel around the bricks to form the rim of the trough.

2) Using a hypertufa mix (see converting a glazed sink), trowel the mix around the bricks, firming it up the sides. Make sure the mixture is not too wet, otherwise it will not cling to the polythene on the sides. Cover the top with 12 mm (½ in) of the mixture, using a float trowel to smooth it.

3) For strength you will have to reinforce the concrete with wire-netting cut to a rectangle that covers the base and over-laps the sides by about 7.5 cm (3 in). You

will need to fold this round the shape
carefully, being sure to make the corners
neat. The netting should lie flat against
the concrete. Cover it with another layer
of hypertufa to give a final thickness of
about 4 cm (1½ in), smoothing it for a
neat finish.

4) For drainage, bore at least five 2.5 cm
(1 in) holes through the base before it
sets. You will also need to scrub the
surface with a stiff brush after about 24
hours, when the mixture has partially set,
so that a matt, more stone-like finish is
produced.

5) After four days you can try lifting the
trough by sliding a spade under the edge
and lifting. It should lift clear of the
bricks, then the polythene can be pulled
off easily.

6) Finish off the trough by making sure
that the drainage holes are clear, and
rounding off the edges of the trough with
a coarse file or shaping tool. This should
be done before the mixture becomes too
hard. Finally, hose it down scrubbing
with a stiff brush. If necessary, weathering can be accelerated by brushing on one
of the mixtures described on page 41.

HOW TO CONVERT A GLAZED SINK

Hypertufa will not stick to a glazed sink
unless you prepare the surface first.
Clean it out thoroughly, making sure the
surface is free of grease or dirt, then try

A sink garden with a collection of over 20
alpines.

to score the glaze on the outside and for a few inches down on the inside. This will not be easy, but you might make some impression with a coarse file. You will not be able to break much of the glaze, but it will help to form a key.

Paint the area to be coated with hypertufa with a PVA adhesive and allow it to become tacky (about 10 minutes). This step is *essential*, otherwise the hypertufa will not stick to the glazed surface.

While the glue is becoming tacky, mix the hypertufa. There are variations on the basic recipe, but a dependable formula is 1 part coarse sand, 1 part cement, and 2 parts moistened sieved sphagnum peat. Mix dry first, then add water until it assumes a doughy consistency.

Wear waterproof gloves and slap on a layer of the mixture, pressing it firmly against the sink. A thickness of 12 mm (½ in) should be adequate. Make sure the hypertufa is taken over the rim and down to below compost level inside. Let the mixture dry out then brush on something to accelerate weathering (see page 41). Do not fill with compost and plant up for at least a week.

SITING

Careful siting is important, both for the sake of the plants and to make the most of the trough or sink as a feature. A sunny position is best, but shade is all right if you are prepared to restrict the plants to those that tolerate it. Avoid, above all, a position under the overhang of trees or bushes, where drips as well as shade are almost certain to be a problem.

Paved areas, perhaps a patio, or a gravelled area generally make a suitable setting. It is best to avoid placing them within a lawn because mowing is likely to be difficult and they can look out of place unless forming a focal point. If you do place the alpine sink or trough on the lawn, lay a small area of paving first, to provide a firm base and to make mowing easier at the edges.

A trough almost always looks better raised off the ground. Failing anything better, just stand it on a couple of loose bricks, but ideally make a proper plinth or legs constructed from bricks or stone. A single pillar or plinth may suffice for a very small trough, but anything large and heavy will need two or three supports.

There is no point in being dogmatic about height; one's view of these things can be influenced by one's own height and sense of 'rightness'. As a guide, the top of the container should be 45−60 cm (1½−2 ft) above the ground. Too high and it can look precarious; too low and it loses its significance.

Always make sure that the drainage holes are not obstructed by the plinth.

PLANTING A TROUGH

For a proper rock garden the amount of compost needed usually dictates that your should mix your own. That is not without its problems, and for the rela-

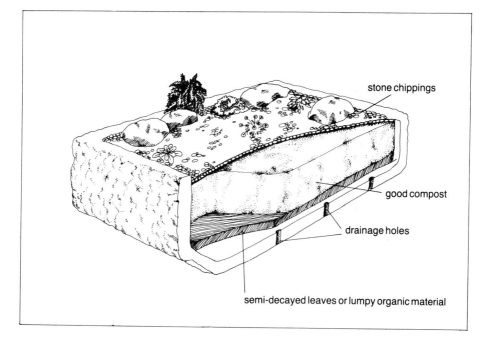

stone chippings

good compost

drainage holes

semi-decayed leaves or lumpy organic material

Troughs, whether natural or man-made, will make an attractive home for a wide range of small and compact alpines.

tively small amount needed for a trough it is much easier to use a loam-based potting compost.

If you are planning to grow lime-hating plants, buy an ericaceous mix. In either case the mixture can be improved by adding up to a third by volume of sharp grit or 6−9 mm (¼−⅜ in) stone chippings. Avoid limestone chipping if you want to grow lime-haters, but otherwise limestone is a good choice. If you want to make up your own compost, follow the advice on page 56.

As always, good drainage is vitally important. Place a piece of perforated zinc or broken crocks (pieces of flower pots) over the drainage holes, then a generous layer of broken pots, gravel, or stone chippings; in a shallow container there will not be room for more than a thin layer, but in deeper troughs you can afford to make the layer a couple of inches deep. Broken pots and other coarse drainage material is best covered with inverted turves before adding the compost. If fine gravel of stone chippings have been used this should not be necessary.

Add the compost, which should be moist but not wet, to the brim, then firm it down so that the finished level is a few inches below the rim.

FINISHING TOUCHES

You will find suggestions for suitable plants in Chapters 7 and 8 and there is a vast selection from which to choose. Plants alone will be attractive, but a few small pieces of rock will often add a finishing touch that makes all the difference.

Because you need only a small amount of rock, it is worth considering tufa or weatherworn limestone, though there is no reason why other rocks should not be used. One or two pieces of reasonable size will usually be far more effective than a sprinkling of small fragments. There is often a reluctance to use large pieces of rock for fear of reducing the space for plants. It does not work that way, because you can plant between the crevices and close to the rocks so that the plants can grow over them. It usually means that relatively little growing space is lost.

Try to build one miniature 'outcrop' of rock rather than dotting the pieces around, and leave planting space at the corners and edges, so that the best use can be made of trailers.

As it is easier to plant in crevices between rocks as you position them, make sure crevice plants are to hand at this stage. Once the trough or sink has been planted, finish off with stone chippings; it will help to keep the necks of the plants out of contact with wet soil, but more importantly it will look better than exposed compost.

GROWING IN TUFA

Tufa is a very unusual type of rock (see page 23), which is porous and easily drilled so that you can insert plants directly into the stone. The larger the piece of tufa the more effective the results as a garden feature.

Some tufa can be hard and flint-like, but other examples can be so soft that it crumbles. Something between the two is ideal. A block about $45 \times 30 \times 30$ cm ($18 \times 12 \times 12$ in) is about the right size; bigger ones look better but are more difficult to handle. Much smaller than this and there could be a problem with the rock drying out too rapidly in summer, and of course it will accommodate fewer plants.

Make the holes with a small cold chisel or an electric drill with a masonry bit that you do not mind sacrificing. Or you could use a brace and bit. The holes should be about 2.5 cm (1 in) wide and $5 - 7.5$ cm ($2 - 3$ in) deep, angled downwards so that the plants are less likely to fall out and to reduce the chances of compost being washed out.

Do not overcrowd the plants, otherwise the decorative effect of the tufa will be lost; it is not necessary to make the holes closer than $10 - 15$ cm ($4 - 6$ in) apart.

Planting Clearly, conventional methods of planting are not practical. You need young plants, perhaps little more than seedlings or rooted cuttings, and you will need to shake most of the compost off the

A single piece of tufa rock can be home for dozens of small choice alpines. The rock is easily drilled to provide small planting pockets (see text).

roots. Roll them in a piece of toilet paper (or other material that will disintegrate when wet), and poke the 'tube' of roots down the hole. A bit of poking from a pencil may help. You may then be able to withdraw the paper without removing the roots, but if you have to leave some of it there it will not matter. Trickle some compost (see below) into the hole, being careful not to squeeze the roots by ramming down hard. Trickle some water down the hole to settle the compost around the roots.

A suitable compost can be made from 2 parts coarse sand, 2 parts leafmould or peat, and 1 part of tufa chippings left from making the holes.

It is best to have the tufa standing on a bed of soil or sand, so that the rock can derive some moisture by capillary action. Tufa standing on paving or stone is likely to dry out quickly. If bedded on sand, keep the sand moist. In summer it will also be necessary to water the stone daily in dry weather, in early morning or late evening. Although the plants will probably prefer full sun, this will hasten the drying process, so if you are unable to water regularly find a position where it is shaded for part of the day. Avoid a very windy position, as this will also hasten drying.

Although tufa is a limestone rock, the lime is not in a form that causes major problems for lime-hating plants. They should grow satisfactorily in tufa, if not quite as well as they might in ideal conditions.

Screes and peat beds have nothing in common; they are put together in this chapter simply because they are specialised forms of rock gardening that enable some of the more demanding alpines to be grown successfully. The scree or moraine provides perfect drainage, ideally coupled with a plentiful supply of water, and the peat bed provides acid conditions for the lime-haters.

Anyone starting with alpines can ignore both screes and peat beds unless they have a visual appeal and fit in particularly well with the garden design. The vast majority of plants will do perfectly well in an ordinary rock garden, and it makes sense to start with the less demanding plants.

Anyone who has already made a start with alpines will undoubtedly reach the stage when the appeal of some of the acid-loving and scree plants demands serious attention. You could always grow them in pots, but if you have the space and setting it is worth giving consideration to a scree and/or a peat garden.

SCREES AND MORAINES

Although screes and moraines are very different things, to most gardeners they are synonymous. They are taken to mean a very free-draining area of gritty, stony ground with very little soil. Strictly speaking, a moraine has a submerged supply of water.

In nature a scree can be regarded as a mass of rock debris and stones with some soil and sand brought down by a glacier and left behind when the ice finally melts. In the rock garden it is usually created as an area towards the foot of a large rock garden, or sometimes as a bed in its own right. A scree often looks most natural sloping very gradually towards a stream or a lower outcrop of rocks. A moraine should be on a fairly steep slope (say 1 in 15) with an underground irrigation system for use in spring and summer.

It is worth being clear about motives if you are considering a scree. If it is just the *appearance* of a scree, stony soil with bits of rock scattered about, you can be less strict in the way you prepare the ground. If you want a scree in order to be able to grow some of the more demanding plants that may not do well in an ordinary rock garden, you will have to be prepared to make a thorough job of the preparation and construction.

Sometimes a low scree bed is used as an alternative to a rock garden, and in some

A scree acting as a link between rock garden and lawn.

settings this may blend in more naturally with the rest of the garden design.

In nature the scree or moraine provides conditions for which some alpine plants are well adapted; snow cover protection in winter, and in spring and early summer ample moisture from melting snow, and a poor but very free-draining soil. These plants often form tight, hard cushions or rosettes, and have long tap roots.

Unless you simply like the appearance of a scree, it is only worth making one if you want to grow those plants that need the exceptionally good drainage and conditions such as impoverished soil to do well.

Excavate the area to a depth of 60 cm (2 ft), and place at least 15 cm (6 in) of

Having constructed an area as free-draining as this, it may seem a paradox to have to make special arrangements for watering, but in spring and summer scree plants must be watered freely. It is worth placing a hidden sprinkler within the bed, laying the hose for this when you construct the bed. Some enthusiasts bury a perforated pipe about 30 cm (1 ft) below the surface, which will supply a trickle of water when the tap is turned on.

Finish the scree off with a few scattered rocks poking through the surface (if the scree is part of a larger rock garden, make sure the rocks match), and dress the surface with gravel or small stone chippings. Be sure, however, to use the right kind of material for the plants to be grown: limestone chippings are ideal for lime-loving plants; granite chippings or gravel will suit the rest.

A scree must be well drained. Here a soakaway has been prepared to ensure adequate drainage.

rubble at the bottom, then cover this with about 15 cm (6 in) of gravel. The rock garden mix described on page 21 can be used to bring the scree up to the surrounding level, but if you plan to grow the more demanding scree plants it is worth making up a special mixture of 6 parts stone chippings, 1 part coarse sand, 1 part peat, and 1 part soil. There are many variations on this mix, and exact proportions are not critical. If made on a slight slope or on a flat area, the finished level of the bed should be about 10 – 13 cm (4 – 5 in) above the surrounding ground.

Planting the scree Chapters 7 and 8 indicate some of the plants that do well on a scree; there are others, of course, and at a pinch most rock garden plants could be used.

Always use young plants, as a vigorous root system is more important than a lot of top growth. Spread the roots out when planting, even if this means losing some of the soil in the root-ball. Be prepared to keep well watered until established.

Try to plant a scree naturally, with perhaps a small group of plants here and a stray one there. Do not overlook the role of a few dwarf shrubs. Avoid over-planting, otherwise the visual effect of the scree will be lost.

PEAT BEDS

A peat bed is really the most sensible way of growing acid-loving plants if you garden on a neutral or alkaline soil. You will have to be careful on an alkaline soil to make sure that the water run-off from the surrounding soil does not affect the acidity of the peat bed. If you garden on chalk, it is best to have the peat garden at the top of the slope rather than at the bottom where limy water may soak into the peat. If there is any risk of that it is probably better to use a peaty soil mixture in an ordinary raised bed (see page 56). If the soil is neutral to start

A peat bed, worth considering if you particularly want to grow a range of acid-loving plants.

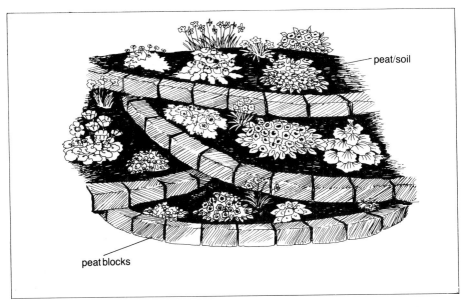

peat/soil

peat blocks

A peat bed can be constructed rather like a rock bed, using peat blocks instead of rocks. A peaty soil mix must be used for the planting pockets.

with you should be able to built a peat garden with peat blocks rather as you might use rocks in a rock garden.

If you have a sloping site, it is best to use peat blocks rather like cliff-type rocks to form terraces up the slope. This is the most natural setting. In a flat garden you may have no choice but to make a more artificial bed, perhaps an island site with a path around it. Examples of both are illustrated below.

Try to obtain specially-cut walling turves, which are more durable than turves cut for fuel. If the blocks are too small, they will tend to break up with handling.

Start the first course an inch or so below the surrounding ground. The wall should ideally be two blocks wide, and of course extra strength will come from bonding like bricks, with staggered joints. Any wall two blocks or more high should always be double-thickness, and if three blocks high place every fourth block of the back row at right angles to bed into the back-fill of peaty soil. A wall 45 cm (1½ ft) or more high should also have a slight backward slope into the bed for extra strength.

Only go up in these steep steps if there is no alternative. The bed will be much more stable, and visually more appealing, if you go up in shorter steps, gaining height by terracing and leaving room for some plants between each step. It is better to have a lower bed gained in small steps than a high bed achieved only at the expense of steep walls.

Peat beds should never be in full sun; most acid-loving plants tend to be shade-lovers anyway, but more importantly you do not want the peat to dry out as it will be very difficult to rewet. A 'shady spot' is not intended to imply that you should place a peat bed beneath the drip of trees. A position perhaps shaded for most of the day by a wall or building might be suitable.

The space behind the peat blocks should be filled with 2 parts moss peat (sedge peat can be used, but it is less satisfactory), 1 part lime-free soil (test it first if necessary, and do not use it if the reading is alkaline), and 1 part sharp sand or grit, all by bulk.

A very peaty mixture has a rather 'fluffy' texture, and it will almost certainly settle during the first week or two. If it does not rain during this time, water it regularly to help the soil mix settle and to ensure that the peat is moist. Top up the beds, if necessary, and then plant.

Obtaining and handling peat blocks
How easy it is to obtain peat blocks will depend on where you live. If you live in an area where peat is cut you are unlikely to have much difficulty – but then you are less likely to be in need of them!

Garden centres *do* stock them, but you may have to phone around first to find one in your area. Some rock garden specialists also stock them. Failing that, it may be possible to order them from a peat supplier and have them delivered if you need a significant quantity.

When you receive them they may be dry, and if so you must soak them thoroughly before using them. As dry peat does not absorb water easily, it is best to immerse them in a tank of water. If you live in an area with a 'hard' (limy) water supply, rain water should be used if possible. Clearly there are times when this is not feasible.

You will soon find that dry blocks float, so be prepared to weight them down; and even then it may take a day or two before the blocks are thoroughly impregnated. Let them drain for a few hours before use.

Planting There will be no trouble planting in the terraces, but do not forget to put some plants in the crevices between the blocks. Plants such as dwarf gaultherias and vacciniums will help to give the walls rigidity by tying them together with their penetrating roots. There are many other plants, especially ferns, that also look good growing in the crevices between blocks.

6·ALPINES IN POTS

It has been said several times already that you do not need a rock garden to grow alpines. You do not even need much of a garden; a greenhouse or even a few cold frames will enable you to grow some really choice alpines in pots.

If it is the plants rather than the rock garden as a feature that appeals, then growing alpines in pots has many advantages. A much wider range of plants can be grown, including many that can be difficult in the open rock garden; they are easier to admire because you can bring them close to eye level, and above all you get to know the plants better.

On the debit side, plants in pots need a lot more attention, such as regular watering at the right season, occasional repotting, and often a lot of moving around from display area to resting or growing area. Although you save on the expense of rocks, you have the cost of greenhouse and frames; and the cost of a large collection of pots is not insignificant.

On balance, it is better to grow your plants in the open garden unless you are prepared for the extra work involved with pot-grown plants. Some of the more difficult plants (those that do not like being wet in winter for instance) need to be grown in pots to do well. Of course if you reach the stage where the exhibition bug bites then you will have to turn to pots.

THE POTS

Plastic pots are fine for raising seedlings; they do not dry out so quickly and therefore need less critical attention, and until the seeds germinate the merits of a clay pot are not evident.

For *growing* alpines, clay pots have many merits. Quite simply they look more 'right' than plastic pots. The porous nature of clay reduces the chances of the plant standing in saturated compost. Clay pots are not without problems. Sometimes they are covered with a green slime when wet (try scrubbing them with permanganate of potash), and often they become covered with a white deposit.

It is possible to buy rectangular clay pots if you feel that you need to pack them in with the minimum of wasted space, but round pots are cheaper and perfectly adequate. The vast majority of alpines will do better and look better in

Alpines in pots enable you to appreciate the plants at close quarters. Many of the more choice alpines are best grown in pots in an alpine house, but even everyday plants such as these *Scilla sibirica* 'Spring Beauty' can be appreciated in pots.

half pots (these are shallower than normal pots), although these are less widely available.

this is part of the fun of the hobby, but do not let mystiques about compost be an obstacle to trying the plants.

THE COMPOST

There are some gardeners who enjoy mixing up special recipes for each plant. It is largely unnecessary and a compromise between this approach and a 'John Innes for everything' philosophy is about right.

Generally, peat-based composts are best avoided. Alpines that you buy in the garden centre may be growing in a peat compost, but that is a commercial marketing decision rather than one based on what is best for the plants in the long-term.

Most alpines will do well in a loam-based compost such as properly made John Innes potting compost No. 1 to which you add 4−6 mm ($^3/16$−¼ in) stone chippings for extra drainage. For acid-loving plants you can buy an ericaceous version (though you may have to shop around for it), and the chippings used should be something like granite rather than limestone. Wash the stone chippings before you use them to get rid of the dust.

For 'scree plants' a mixture of equal parts stone chippings and a loam-based compost without lime (an ericaceous mix) is likely to satisfy most of them.

There are lots of other compost mixtures that you can experiment with, and once you have a basic collection of plants

POTTING-ON AND REPOTTING

Because terms such as potting-up and repotting can lead to confusion, as they can mean different things to different people, it is worth a paragraph to define what is meant here. In this book potting-up applies to potting young seedlings or rooted cuttings for the first time. Potting-on is moving the plant on from one pot into a larger one. Repotting is often taken to mean moving into a larger pot, but in this book it means repotting in the same-sized pot with fresh compost. This is most likely to be applicable for plants with tap roots or thongy roots. You may be able to take the opportunity to take root cuttings while repotting these plants. It is worth making an annual event of potting-on or repotting. Early summer or mid-summer is generally a convenient time.

There is a lot to be said for moving most plants into a clean pot, even if it does not need moving up or the compost changed. It will give you a chance to keep the pots clean. Soak the old pots in a large container of water (an old dustbin is often convenient) with washing soda added, then scrub them clean. A scrubbing brush dipped in silver sand is often successful as the sand acts as an abrasive. It is a good idea to soak new pots in water for a few hours before you use them.

Do not be in too much of a hurry to repot established alpines. Young plants may need more frequent repotting. The method being used here is to pack the compost in the new pot round the existing pot (or one of the same size) to form a mould. The plant will fit snugly into the space when removed from the pot, and the compost will need only light firming round the root-ball.

If the plant does not really need repotting or potting-on, and you are just replacing in a fresh pot of the same size, this is your opportunity to remove any layer of moss on the surface of the compost, and to renew the topdressing of chippings if necessary. Generally a plant will need potting-on if the soil-ball is full of roots twisting around the inside of the pot.

AN ALPINE HOUSE

Although the term greenhouse has been used so far, alpines are best grown in an alpine house; this is a greenhouse designed with alpines in mind. Ideally it has a lower-pitched roof than a traditional greenhouse, but this is much less important than the ventilation. An alpine house will have many more ventilators than a normal greenhouse, in the roof and on both sides. There are likely to be ventilators at staging height too. An ordinary greenhouse can be adapted by incorporating additional roof vents and plenty of louvre ventilators in the sides.

As the pots will undoubtedly look

The old alpine house at the Royal Horticultural Society's garden at Wisley, in Surrey, England, where there are plants in flower every month of the year.

better plunged in gravel in a deep bench, you may need to shop around for suitable staging. Staging supplied for an ordinary greenhouse is unlikely to be suitable.

An alpine greenhouse is never heated, and the ventilators should be open most of the time, only being closed to avoid excessive rain or very cold winds blowing directly into the house.

Shading is necessary in summer. External roller blinds are ideal but expensive; strips of muslin wired to the inside that you can pull back are practical and inexpensive. A white external shading wash is very effective and not costly, but you have the sometimes tedious job of removing it at the end of the season.

An alpine frame. Although something for the specialist, you may find this an acceptable alternative if you do not have a greenhouse.

FRAMES

Cold frames are much more inconvenient than a greenhouse, but the plants will be happy enough. Certainly if you want to use your greenhouse mainly for display,

you will need frames for the plants that are not at an attractive stage. Bring the plants into the greenhouse while they are at their most attractive, and move them back to the frame when they are not.

As with a greenhouse, a frame must be ventilated freely at all times, and shaded during the summer.

7·BASIC ALPINES

Although relatively long, this chapter represents only a small proportion of the plants that you could grow, and any specialist alpine catalogue will contain many more. The plants in this chapter are those that you are likely to find in garden centres, although the range stocked will vary enormously from one garden centre to the next, and will vary with season. It does not contain the very many more specialised alpines that an enthusiast would probably want to try, nor alpines that really need scree or alpine house conditions. However, a longer list of plants would be likely to bewilder all but the already dedicated enthusiast.

The propagation advice does not include all the methods that might be possible, only those that you are most likely to use. There is little point in using a more difficult or troublesome method if a simpler one will do. The choice between seed and cuttings is a more difficult one; seed gives you the chance to raise perhaps more plants, but often more slowly, cuttings (and other vegetative means such as division) will guarantee that the offspring are like the parent even if the plant is a variety or hybrid. Sometimes one method rather than another will suit a particular need.

Use the flowering and foliage seasons at the top of each entry to ensure that you have pockets of colour over a long period. One of the criticisms often made of rock gardens is that everything happens in spring and early summer and the garden is dull for the rest of the year. Selecting plants to flower or hold interest at other times of the year will overcome this problem.

PERENNIAL ALPINES

Acaena buchananii (New Zealand burr) *Decorative fruits* Late summer to early autumn. *Uses* Full sun; ground cover; between paving; in wall.

This is a mat-forming plant with silvery green briar-like foliage. It has insignificant flowers and yellowish burr-like fruits. It provides ground cover among dwarf bulbs. Divide in spring. 2.5 – 5 cm (1 – 2 in).

Acaena microphylla (New Zealand burr) *Decorative fruits* Late summer to early autumn. *Uses* Full sun; ground cover; between paving; in wall.

A flat, spreading carpet with grey pinnate leaves, sometimes shading to reddish-brown, it has attractive spiny,

Acaena microphylla.

Aethionema 'Warley Ruber'.

globular, crimson burrs. Divide in spring. 2.5 – 5 cm (1 – 2 in).

Achillea 'King Edward' (yarrow, milfoil) *Flowering season* Late spring to early autumn. *Uses* Full sun; between paving; in wall.

This is a free-flowering garden hybrid of *A. clavennae*, which may be listed as *A. lewisii*. The primrose-yellow flowers last over a long period. Finely divided foliage. Increase by division in spring or early autumn. 15 cm (6 in).

Achillea tomentosa *Flowering season* Early to late summer. *Uses* Full sun; between paving; in wall.

This plant has mats of woolly, ferny

leaves topped with flat heads of mustard-yellow flowers. Divide in spring. 20 cm (8 in).

Aethionema 'Warley Rose' *Flowering season* Late spring. *Uses* Full sun; trough or sink; in wall.

This variety has a bushy, compact habit, blue-grey leaves and intense pink flower heads. Take cuttings in summer. 15 cm (6 in).

Ajuga reptans (bugle) *Flowering season* Late spring. *Foliage season* Mid-spring to early autumn. *Uses* Partial shade; ground cover; herbaceous border; between paving.

Bugle makes a spreading mat of glossy,

61

Ajuga reptans.

Alyssum saxatile.

coloured or variegated rosettes. 'Burgundy Glow' is a popular variety; it has crinkled leaves variegated pink, bronze and cream. Blue flowers appear on short spikes. It has a spreading habit, and can be invasive. It likes a moist position. Divide from spring to autumn. 10 cm (4 in).

Alyssum montanum *Flowering season* Late spring to early summer. *Uses* Full sun; between paving; in wall.

This plant has a creeping habit, grey-green leaves and loose heads of bright yellow flowers with notched petals. It can be rather rampant, but looks good on a sunny bank with aubrietas. Sow seed in early spring, or take cuttings in early summer. 13 cm (5 in).

Alyssum saxatile (gold dust) *Flowering season* Mid-spring to early summer.

Uses Full sun; herbaceous border; in wall.

Although one of the most widely grown rock plants, it is too rampant to grow among choice plants. It has evergreen grey-green leaves. The plant is covered with heads of yellow flower from mid-spring. Colours range from deep yellow to pale buff-yellow according to variety. Sow seed in early spring, or take cuttings in early summer. 23 – 30 cm (9 – 12 in). 'Compactum' grows to 15 cm (6 in).

Alyssum spinosum *Flowering season* Late spring to early summer. *Uses* Full sun.

Now more correctly called *Ptilotrichum*

spinosum, this shrublet has fine spines, and clusters of small pale deep rose flowers. Sow seed in autumn or transplant self-sown seedlings. 10–20 cm (4–8 in).

Anacyclus depressus *Flowering season* Early to late summer. *Uses* Full sun.

This plant has flat rosettes of finely divided, feathery leaves, and white daisy flowers, reddish beneath. It dislikes being wet in winter. Sow seed; prechill if sown in spring. 20 cm (8 in).

Androsace sarmentosa (rock jasmine) *Flowering season* Early to midsummer. *Uses* Full sun; trough or sink; in wall.

This is a mat-forming plant with small rosettes of slightly hairy leaves from which arise umbels of pink flowers. It spreads quickly. Raise from seed sown in late winter (prechill) or divide. 15 cm (6 in).

Antennaria alpina (cat's ear) *Flowering season* Mid- to late summer. *Uses* Full sun.

This is a carpeting plant with short, tufty grey-green leaves, and clusters of pale pink flowers. Divide in spring or early autumn. 10 cm (4 in).

Antennaria dioica *Flowering season* Late spring to early summer. *Uses* Full sun; between paving.

This plant forms a dense mat of creeping stems. It has silvery leaves, and upright stems with pretty tufted flowers

Androsace sarmentosa.

Aquilegia alpina.

from white to deep pink. 'Rosea' and 'Rubra' are popular varieties. Divide in early spring. 10 cm (4 in).

Aquilegia alpina (columbine) *Flowering season* Late spring. *Uses* Partial shade.

Columbine has dissected grey-green leaves, and blue or blue-and-white flowers, about 5 cm (2 in) long. Sow fresh seed in mid-summer; sow old seed in spring. 30 cm (1 ft).

Arabis caucasica (rock cress) *Flowering season* Early spring to early summer. *Uses* Full sun; herbaceous border; in wall.

This may still be listed as *A. albida*. It has grey-green hoary leaves, and masses of white flowers, although the best form (because it is less rampant) is 'Rosabella', which has pink flowers. It is best among other strong-growers such as *Alyssum saxatile* and aubrieta. Raise from seed, or divide in early autumn. 23 cm (9 in).

Arabis ferdinandi-coburgi 'Variegata' *Flowering season* Mid- to late spring. *Foliage season* All year. *Uses* Full sun; trough or sink.

This is a hummock-forming plant with variegated leaves. The white flowers are a bonus in spring. Divide in autumn or early spring. 10 cm (4 in).

Arenaria balearica (sandwort) *Flowering season* Mid-spring to late summer. *Uses* Partial shade; between paving; in wall.

This is a creeping moss-like plant that

Arabis caucasica.

will cover rocks in moist shade with tiny white star-like flowers all summer. It is sometimes killed in a severe winter. Divide in early autumn. 2.5 cm (1 in).

Arenaria montana (sandwort) *Flowering season* Late spring to late summer. *Uses* Full sun.

Sandwort forms a loose mat of wiry, scrambling stems, and has large white flowers. It is easily raised from seed sown in spring, or by division in autumn. 15 cm (6 in).

Armeria maritima (thrift) *Flowering season* Early summer to early autumn. *Uses* Full sun; between paving; in wall.

This plant has tufts of evergreen, grass-like foliage. The showy flower heads are carried clear of the leaves. Colours vary from white through pink to almost red.

Armeria in stone sink.

Sow seed in spring or take cuttings in mid summer. 15 cm (6 in).

Aster alpinus *Flowering season* Late spring to early summer. *Uses* Full sun; trough or sink.

This is a neat, clump-forming species with yellow-centred daisy flowers in shades from pinkish lilac to blue, also white. It can be rather spreading. Increase by division. 15 – 20 cm (6 – 8 in).

Astilbe chinensis pumila *Flowering season* Late summer to early autumn. *Uses* Full sun or partial shade.

This plant has divided foliage and rather stiff but fluffy narrow lilac-pink flower spikes. It is best in moist soil. Divide in spring. 20 – 25 cm (8 – 10 in).

Aubrieta deltoidea *Flowering season* Early spring to early summer. *Uses* Alkaline soil; full sun; herbaceous border; in wall.

One of the most popular rock plants, this plant can be invasive and needs trimming back after flowering. Named varieties are likely to have better colours than seed-raised plants. Colours include shades of red, purple and blue. Seed or cuttings. 8 – 10 cm (3 – 4 in).

Campanula carpatica *Flowering season* Early to late summer. *Uses* Full sun or partial shade; trough or sink.

Upturned cupped or bowl-shaped flowers are produced above bushy growth. Colours include shades of blue, and white, according to variety. 'Blue Clips' and 'White Clips' are widely available varieties. Seed or division in spring. 10 – 15 cm (4 – 6 in).

Campanula cochleariifolia *Flowering season* Early to late summer. *Uses* Full sun or partial shade; between paving.

This plant has fresh green leaves and masses of little bells on slender branched stems. There are shades of blue, also white. It is spreading but not difficult to control. Seed. Increase is easy by division in early spring. 8 cm (3 in).

Campanula garganica *Flowering season* Early to late summer. *Uses* Full sun; between paving.

This plant has a rosette of small, ivy-shaped leaves and arching sprays of starry blue flowers. Seed or division. 8 cm (3 in).

Cerastium tomentosum (snow in summer) *Flowering season* Late spring to

Aubrieta 'Henslow Purple'.

Campanula carpatica.

early summer. *Foliage season* All year. *Uses* Full sun; in wall.

This is a spreading, rather rampant evergreen grey-leaved plant with masses of white flowers. It is too vigorous for the rock garden, but useful for wall planting or clothing banks. It is easily propagated by seed or division in spring. 10–15 cm (4–6 in).

Corydalis lutea *Flowering season* Mid-spring to mid-autumn. *Uses* Full sun or full shade.

This plant has feathery fern-like foliage, and yellow flowers over a long period. Most useful as a wall plant. Self-sows freely. 15 cm (6 in).

Cotyledon simplicifolia *Flowering season* Early to mid-summer. *Uses* Full sun or full shade; in wall.

More correctly called *Chiastophyllum oppositifolium*, this is an impressive rock plant, but it needs a moist position. It has rosettes of fleshy leaves, and drooping sprays of small yellow flowers. Increase by division. 15 cm (6 in).

Crepis aurea *Flowering season* Early to mid-summer. *Uses* Full sun.

This plant has leafy clumps of dandelion-type foliage, and burnt orange dandelion-like flowers. It tends to become weedy-looking. Sow seed or divide in spring. 23 cm (9 in).

Dianthus deltoides (maiden pink) *Flowering season* Early to late summer. *Uses* Alkaline soil; full sun; herbaceous border; between paving; in wall.

Dianthus deltoides has linear evergreen leaves, and pink to red, sometimes white, single flowers about 12 mm (½ in) across. There are named varieties such as 'Flashing Light' (bright crimson), and 'Pikes Pink' (pink, semi-double). Sow

Cotyledon simplicifolia.

Diascia cordata.

seed or take cuttings after flowering. 15 – 23 cm (6 – 9 in).

Diascia cordata *Flowering season* Early summer to early autumn. *Uses* Full sun.

This may be sold as *D. cordifolia*. It has a cushion of dark glossy leaves, and prostrate, spreading shoots with sprays of comparatively large pink, spurred flowers. Divide every few years to keep vigorous. 15 – 25 cm (6 – 10 in).

Draba aizoides *Flowering season* Early to late spring. *Uses* Full sun.

This species has deep green rosettes of rigid brittle-tipped leaves, and bunches of loose-petalled lemon-yellow flowers. Propagate by seed or division. 10 cm (4 in).

Dryas octopetala, showing the attractive seed heads.

Dryas octopetala *Flowering season* Late spring to mid-summer. *Uses* Full sun; herbaceous border; between paving.

This is a mat-forming plant, with evergreen leaves deep green above, silvery beneath. The white flowers have a yellow centre, over 2.5 cm (1 in) across, followed by fluffy white seed heads. Propagate by seed or division. *D. × suendermannii* is similar but more free-flowering. 5 cm (2 in).

Erinus alpinus *Flowering season* Late spring to mid-summer. *Uses* Full sun; between paving; in wall.

Erinus has tufts of evergreen, almost fern-like leaves, and a profusion of small bright pink flowers on wiry stems. Although generally short-lived it self-seeds freely. The type has lilac-mauve flowers, but there are other colours which include pink and white. It is a good crevice plant. Sow where it is to flower. 8 cm (3 in).

Frankenia thymifolia (sea heath) *Flowering season* Early summer to early autumn. *Uses* Full sun.

This ground-hugging plant with spiny greenish-bronze foliage has pale pink flowers. It prefers dry soil. Take cuttings in summer or divide in spring. 2.5 cm (1 in).

Gentiana acaulis (trumpet gentian)
Flowering season Late spring to early summer. *Uses* Full sun; trough or sink.

This plant produces a clumpy growth of evergreen rosettes, and vivid blue trumpet-shaped flowers, which are not always produced as freely as one would like. Increase by divison in early summer. 10 cm (4 in).

Gentiana septemfida *Flowering season* Mid- to late summer. *Uses* Full sun.

This gentian has compact tufts of mid green leaves and clusters of deep blue flowers. It is best raised from ripe seed sown in autumn. 20 cm (8 in).

Gentiana septemfida.

Gentiana sino-ornata *Flowering season* Early to mid-autumn. *Uses* Acid soil; full sun or partial shade.

The brilliant blue flowers are striped deep blue and greenish-yellow. Divide in early spring or take cuttings from mid-summer to early autumn. 10 cm (4 in).

Geranium sanguineum 'Lancastriense' *Flowering season* Early to late summer. *Uses* Full sun; herbaceous border.

This plant forms mats of soft, lobed leaves, and has a semi-prostrate habit. The rose-pink flowers are about 2.5 cm (1 in) across. Increase by division. 15–23 cm (6–9 in).

Geranium subcaulescens *Flowering season* Early to late summer. *Uses* Full sun; herbaceous border.

Grey-green lobed leaves, a trailing habit and rich crimson flowers with a dark eye are the features of this plant. Increase by division. 15 cm (6 in).

Gypsophila repens *Flowering season* Early to late summer. *Uses* Alkaline soil; full sun; herbaceous border; in wall.

This is a branching, rather sprawling plant with wiry stems. It has grey-green leaves in pairs, and masses of small flowers from white to pink. 'Rosea' is a pink form often grown. Take cuttings in spring. 15 cm (6 in).

Helichrysum bellidioides *Flowering season* Early to late summer. *Uses* Full sun.

This prostrate carpeter can become rampant. It has woolly silvery leaves and heads of white 'everlasting' daisy-like flowers. It may need winter protection. Increase by division. 10 cm (4 in).

Geranium subcaulescens.

Leontopodium alpinum (edelweiss)
Flowering season Late spring to mid-summer. *Uses* Full sun.

Edelweiss has narrow, lanceolate, greyish leaves and curious irregularly star-shaped white flowers. It is generally short-lived. Propagate from seed. 20 cm (8 in).

Lychnis alpina *Flowering season* Late spring to mid-summer. *Uses* Full sun; in wall.

This plant produces tufts of dark green linear leaves, and heads of five-petalled flowers. These are usually deep rose, but the colour is variable. Propagate from seeds or cuttings. 10 cm (4 in).

Mazus reptans *Flowering season* Early

Gypsophila repens 'Letchworth Rose'.

Oxalis adenophylla.

Helichrysum bellidioides.

to mid-summer. *Uses* Partial shade; ground cover; between paving.

This is a rapid spreader with bronze-green leaves and lipped, mimulus-like mauve flowers. It may become straggly with age. It is suitable as a ground cover plant over bulbs. It is easily raised from seed or cuttings. 5 cm (2 in).

Micromeria corsica *Flowering season* Mid- to late summer. *Uses* Full sun.

This makes a small silvery-grey hummock with tiny pink, lavender-scented flowers. Divide in spring. 5 cm (2 in).

Mimulus × burnetii 'A.T. Johnson' *Flowering season* Early to late summer. *Uses* Full sun or partial shade.

This variety has large deep yellow lipped trumpet-shaped flowers mottled browny-red. It will tolerate a drier position than most mimulus, but still

Phlox subulata 'Alexander's Surprise'.

prefers a moist soil. It is easily raised from cuttings. 20 cm (8 in).

Oxalis adenophylla *Flowering season* Late spring to early summer. *Uses* Full sun.

Oxalis forms a cushion of grey-green divided foliage, topped with lilac-pink funnel-shaped flowers. To propagate, divide the fibre-coated bulb-like rhizome. 10 cm (4 in).

Penstemon pinifolius *Flowering season* Mid-summer to early autumn. *Uses* Full sun.

This plant has an erect growth but rather spreading habit. It has narrow leaves and sprays of scarlet very narrow, tubular flowers. Propagate from seed or take cuttings in mid- or late summer. 15 – 23 cm (6 – 9 in).

Phlox douglasii *Flowering season* Mid- to late spring. *Uses* Full sun; trough or sink; in wall.

This is a carpeting plant, rooting as it spreads. Masses of flowers about 12 – 18 mm (½ – ¾ in) across. The colour range includes lilac, pale blue, pink to red, and white. There are many named varieties, including 'Boothman's Variety' (mauve with violet-purple centre), 'Crackerjack' (the best red), 'Eva' (pink), 'May Snow' (white), and 'Rosea' (pink). Propagate these from cuttings. 5 – 10 cm (2 – 4 in).

Phlox   subulata   (moss   phlox) *Flowering season* Mid- to late spring. *Uses* Full sun; in wall.

This phlox is similar to *P. douglasii*, but generally has brighter colours, and spreading mats of linear leaves. Named varieties include 'G.F. Wilson' (a good light blue) and 'Scarlet Flame' (bright red). Propagate named varieties from cuttings. 5 – 10 cm (2 – 4 in).

Polygonum vacciniifolium.

Polygonum vacciniifolium *Flowering season* Late summer to mid-autumn. *Uses* Full sun; herbaceous border; in wall.

This plant forms a spreading evergreen mat, and can be invasive in the wrong place. It has small pink 'poker' flowers. Divide in early spring. 15 cm (6 in).

Potentilla × tonguei *Flowering season* Mid- to late summer. *Uses* Full sun.

These clumpy plants have dark green branching stems and striking apricot-coloured flowers with a crimson blotch. To increase stock, divide in early spring. 20–25 cm (8–10 in).

Potentilla tabernaemontani *Flowering season* Late spring to mid-summer. *Uses* Full sun; trough or sink.

More correctly called *P. neumanniana*, this plant is more likely to be found under its old name of *P. verna*. 'Nana' is the variety to grow in the rock garden. It has bright green mounds studded with bold yellow buttercup-like flowers. Divide in spring or autumn, or take cuttings in spring. 10 cm (4 in).

Primula auricula (auricula) *Flowering season* Mid- to late spring. *Uses* Full sun or partial shade.

This primula has flat rosettes of fleshy oval leaves, usually heavily powdered with farina. The species has umbels of yellow flowers, but it is usually the large-flowered mixtures that are grown, and these include blue and red colourings. Increase by seed or by division in late summer. 15 cm (6 in).

Primula denticulata.

Primula denticulata (drumstick primula) *Flowering season* Early to late spring. *Uses* Partial shade; herbaceous border.

This species has globular heads topping stiff stems. The colours range from lilac through violet, pink, crimson and purple to pure white. It is best in moist, rich soil. Divide in late summer or sow seed in late spring or early summer. Root cuttings can also be used. 30 cm (1 ft).

Primula rosea *Flowering season* Early to late spring. *Uses* Partial shade.

This compact, tuft-forming plant has umbels of intense rose-pink flowers. It is best in a damp position. It is easy to propagate from seed, but divide in early autumn to keep true. 15 cm (6 in).

Pulsatilla vulgaris.

Pulsatilla vulgaris (Pasque flower)

Flowering season Mid-spring. *Uses* Alkaline soil; full sun; herbaceous border.

This plant has finely divided, ferny foliage, and striking lavender-purple flowers, although there are red, pink, and white forms. It is a beautiful and long-lived alpine. There are attractive fluffy seed heads. Raise from seed, if possible sown as soon as it is ripe. 20–30 cm (8–12 in).

Raoulia australis *Foliage season* All year. *Uses* Full sun; between paving; trough or sink.

This is now considered to be *R. hookeri*, which is separately listed in some catalogues as a distinct species. It forms a spreading evergreen mat of tiny, silvery rosettes. The flowers are insignificant. Propagate by division. 12 mm (½ in).

Saponaria ocymoides *Flowering season* Late spring to mid-summer. *Uses* Full sun; herbaceous border; in wall.

Raoulia australis.

This is a vigorous, prostrate plant with bright pink flowers. It is not long-lived but self-seeds prolifically. 'Compacta' is slower-growing and more compact. It is easily grown from seed, but the plants may be variable. They can be divided from mid-autumn to early spring. 15 cm (6 in).

Saxifraga aizoon *Flowering season* Late spring to early summer. *Uses* Alkaline soil; full sun or partial shade; tufa block, trough or sink.

Now more correctly called *S. paniculata*, you will still find this plant in most catalogues as *S. aizoon*. It is a very variable species, but usually has rosettes of widely or narrowly strap-shaped grey-green leaves. They are often encrusted with dots of lime, particularly around the edges. It forms mats with short stolons,

and has white, yellow or pink flowers, depending on the variety. It is best propagated by cuttings of individual rosettes after flowering. 15 – 25 cm (6 – 10 in).

Saxifraga × apiculata *Flowering season* Early to mid-spring. *Uses* Partial shade; trough or sink.

This plant has tight cushions of narrow, hoary green leaves and yellow flowers, although there is a white variety ('Alba'). Treat non-flowering rosettes as cuttings in early summer. 10 cm (4 in).

Saxifraga cotyledon *Flowering season* Early to late summer. *Uses* Full sun or partial shade.

The rosettes of strap-shaped dark green leaves are lime-encrusted at the margins. There are plume-like sprays of white flowers. Treat non-flowering rosettes as cuttings. 45 – 60 cm (1½ – 2 ft).

Saxifraga × apiculata.

Saxifraga, mossy types *Flowering season* Mid- to late spring. *Uses* Partial shade; trough or sink.

These have been grouped together because there are many good hybrids in this section, and often they are sold in garden centres without a specific name. They form dense hummocks of deeply divided leaves, having a moss-like appearance from a distance. Two of the best hybrids are 'Peter Pan' (clear pink flowers) and 'Pixie' (deep red). Divide after flowering or use non-flowering rosettes as cuttings. 5 – 8 cm (2 – 3 in).

Sedum acre *Flowering season* Early to late summer.

This plant cannot be recommended. No matter how attractive it looks, especially in the variety 'Aureum', it will almost certainly become a persistent weed in the garden once introduced. Even tiny fragments of the plant will root, and eradicating it from a rock garden can be extremely tedious.

Sedum album *Flowering season* Early to mid-summer. *Uses* Full sun; in wall.

This mat-forming evergreen alpine with oblong cylindrical leaves has clusters of white flowers. It is best in a hot, dry position. 5 – 10 cm (2 – 4 in).

Sedum floriferum 'Weihenstephaner Gold' *Flowering season* Mid- to late summer. *Uses* Full sun.

This sedum has dark leaves, bright yellow flowers. Propagate by division or from cuttings. 10 – 15 cm (4 – 6 in).

Sedum lydium.

Sedum hispanicum *Flowering season* Early to mid-summer. *Uses* Full sun.

This sedum makes a spreading mat of short, prostrate stems with blue-grey foliage, and has white flowers. It dies back to a mass of tangled twigs in winter. Divide between autumn and spring, or raise from seed. 5 cm (2 in).

Sedum lydium *Flowering season* Early to mid-summer. *Uses* Full sun; trough or sink.

This species forms a mass of spreading stems, which root easily as they come into contact with the soil. It has narrowly cylindrical leaves, often bronzed or tinged red, and heads of small white flowers. Divide in early autumn. 5 – 8 cm (2 – 3 in).

Sedum middendorfianum *Flowering season* Early to mid-summer. *Uses* Alkaline soil; full sun.

More correctly called *S. kamtschaticum middendorfianum*, this species has yellow flowers. It can be invasive. Divide in early autumn or early spring, or take cuttings in early summer. 15 cm (6 in).

Sedum spathulifolium *Flowering season* Early to mid-summer. *Foliage season* All year. *Uses* Full sun.

Dense mats of overlapping flat rosettes of spoon-shaped evergreen leaves are formed and there are attractive heads of yellow starry flowers. Two forms with

Sempervivella alba.

particularly attractive foliage are 'Capablanca', often spelt 'Cappa Blanca', (grey leaves) and 'Purpureum' (purple leaves). Easily divided, but cuttings are an alternative. 5 – 10 cm (2 – 4 in).

Sempervivella alba *Flowering season* Late summer to early autumn. *Uses* Full sun; trough or sink.

This plant has a cushion of red-tinged sempervivum-like rosettes, and sprays of

Sempervivums on roof.

Sisyrinchium.

relatively large white, star-shaped flowers. Divide in early autumn or early spring, or take cuttings in late summer. Easily raised from seed, but it may need protection. 5 cm (2 in).

Sempervivum arachnoideum (cobweb houseleek) *Flowering season* Early to mid-summer. *Uses* Full sun; trough or sink; in wall.

This species has tightly-packed globular rosettes, the leaves sometimes flushed red. The tips are woven together with a white mat of cobweb-like hairs. The subspecies *S.a. tomentosum*, usually sold under the name *S.a. laggeri*, has larger rosettes and is particularly densely webbed. It has rose-red flowers. To increase the stock, just remove rooted offsets. 15 cm (6 in).

Sempervivum tectorum (houseleek) *Flowering season* Mid-summer. *Foliage season* All year. *Uses* Full sun; trough or sink; in wall.

This plant has large rosettes, usually about 5 – 8 cm (2 – 3 in) across, occasionally larger. The leaves are usually purple-tipped. It is a very variable species, with many varieties and hybrids. Rose-purple flowers are carried well above the rosettes. The height given below is for flowering heads; the rosettes are only 5 – 8 cm (2 – 3 in) high. To increase stock, simply remove rooted offsets. 15 – 30 cm (6 – 12 in).

Silene acaulis (moss campion) *Flowering season* Late spring. *Uses* Full sun; between paving; trough or sink.

This plant forms a dense mat of narrow

Veronica prostrata.

glossy green leaves. It has five-petalled vivid pink flowers, but is often reluctant to produce them. The colour is sometimes pale pink or even white. Take cuttings in mid- or late summer. 2.5 – 5 cm (1 – 2 in).

Silene schafta *Flowering season* Midsummer to early autumn. *Uses* Full sun; in wall.

This is a tufty plant of spreading habit, which forms a low green clump, topped with magenta-pink flowers over a long season. Sow seed in spring, or take cuttings in mid-summer. It is rather vigorous. 15 cm (6 in).

Sisyrinchium brachypus *Flowering season* Early summer to mid-autumn. *Uses* Full sun.

This plant has sword-shaped leaves, and bright yellow, star-like flowers. Divide or sow seed; both methods are easy and quick. 15 cm (6 in).

Solidago brachystachys *Flowering season* Late summer to early autumn. *Uses* Full sun.

This is a compact, clumpy plant with lanceolate leaves, and plumes of tiny golden-yellow flowers. Division is the simplest form of propagation. 15 cm (6 in).

Thymus × citriodorus 'Aureus' (lemon-scented thyme) *Flowering season* Early to late summer. *Foliage season* Best mid-spring to early autumn. *Uses* Full sun; in wall.

This is a shrublet with gold leaves, which tends to revert to green. It has pale lilac flowers. Take heel cuttings in mid-summer. 23 – 30 cm (9 – 12 in).

Thymus serpyllum (thyme) *Flowering season* Early to late summer. *Uses* Full sun; between paving; in wall.

Now considered to be *T. drucei*, this prostrate, carpeting plant forms a dense mat of thread-like branches. It has tiny oval leaves, and is covered with tiny flowers in summer. The species is very variable and there are several varieties, including 'Albus' (white), 'Coccineus' (deep red), and 'Pink Chintz' (rich rose). Division in early spring or early autumn is an easy method of propagation. 2.5 – 8 cm (1 – 3 in).

Tunica saxifraga *Flowering season* Mid-summer to early autumn. *Uses* Full sun; in wall.

This plant has tufts of linear foliage, and small pale pink star-like flowers on branching wiry stems. It is rather short-lived. Sow seed in late winter or take cuttings in late spring. 15 cm (6 in).

Veronica prostrata *Flowering season* Early to mid-summer. *Uses* Full sun.

This is a mat-forming plant with a trailing habit, and spikes of deep blue flowers. 'Blue Sheen' and 'Spode Blue' are good varieties. 'Mrs Holt' is pink. Propagate by division or from cuttings taken in mid- or late summer. 10 – 15 cm (4 – 6 in).

Viola pedatifida *Flowering season* Mid- to late spring. *Uses* Partial shade.

The blue flowers tend to become lost among the foliage. Self-sown seedlings can become a nuisance. It is easy to propagate from seed. 10 cm (4 in).

BULBS AND CORMS

It is easy to overlook bulbs when buying rock garden plants. They can be just as desirable as any of the herbaceous and evergreen alpine plants, and it is worth finding room for at least some of those described below, whether you have a generously-sized rock garden, an alpine house, or a single sink or trough.

The term 'bulb' has been used loosely. Corms and tubers have also been included. All the bulbs, corms and tubers mentioned here are available from good bulb merchants or specialist bulb suppliers.

Bulb catalogues will offer many more

plants that are suitable for a rock garden, but be cautious as not all dwarf bulbs look right in a rock garden; some of the modern hybrids can look far too garish and out of keeping, though they may be perfectly desirable for another setting.

Although all the bulbs below can be grown from seed (varieties are unlikely to come true from seed), it is often a slow process, and it is usually quicker and easier to divide established clumps or to remove offset bulbs or cormlets and grow these on in a nursery bed for a year or two before planting out again.

Allium karataviense *Flowering season* Late spring to early summer. *Uses* Full sun.

This plant is on the large side for a rock garden, but compact and worth considering. It has broad leaves with a metallic lustre and a narrow red margin. The larger globular flower heads are lilac-white to mauve. 15 – 20 cm (6 – 8 in).

Allium moly *Flowering season* Early summer. *Uses* Full sun.

Allium karataviense.

This species has glaucous leaves, and bold umbels of golden-yellow flowers. It tends to have a rather straggly habit. 25 cm (10 in).

Allium oreophilum *Flowering season* Early to mid-summer. *Uses* Full sun.

This may sometimes be listed as *A. ostrowskianum*. It has globular heads of carmine-pink flowers. 10 – 15 cm (4 – 6 in).

Allium sphaerocephalum *Flowering season* Early to mid-summer. *Uses* Full sun.

With compact, almost cone-shaped, heads of crimson-maroon flowers, this plant is on the borderline of being too tall for a rock garden. 60 cm (2 ft).

Anemone blanda *Flowering season* Early to mid-spring. *Uses* Sun or shade.

This anemone has daisy-like flowers over a carpet of feathery green leaves. The flowers are purple-blue, although there are other separate colours, and mixtures containing shades of blue and pink as well as white. A single colour is most effective. 10 – 15 cm (4 – 6 in).

Arisarum proboscideum (mouse plant) *Flowering season* Late spring. *Uses* Leafy woodland soil; full shade.

This is a tuberous plant with deep green arrow-shaped leaves. The small arum-like spathe terminates in a curved tail about 8 cm (3 in) long, giving rise to the common name. It is best in a woodland-type soil. 8 – 10 cm (3 – 4 in).

Bulbocodium vernum *Flowering season* Early to mid-spring. *Uses* Full sun.

The rosy-violet cup-shaped flowers are rather like those of an autumn crocus (colchicum). Strap-shaped leaves follow the flowers. 5 – 10 cm (2 – 4 in).

Chionodoxa luciliae (glory of the snow) *Flowering season* Early to mid-spring. *Uses* Full sun.

This is one of the easiest small bulbs, with delicate sprays of six-petalled starry blue flowers shading to white in the centre. Pink varieties are also available, but the blue usually looks better. 10 – 15 cm (4 – 6 in).

Chionodoxa among heathers.

Crocus speciosus.

Colchicum autumnale *Flowering season* Late summer to mid-autumn. *Uses* Full sun.

This species has large, crocus-shaped pink flowers, which appear before the leaves. It is useful for late colour. 13 – 15 cm (5 – 6 in).

Colchicum speciosum *Flowering season* Early to mid-autumn. *Uses* Full sun.

The large, goblet-shaped 'crocus' flowers appear before the leaves. The foliage, which is rather coarse, appears in spring. Colour varies from deep purple-rose to white. There are double varieties. 20 – 25 cm (8 – 10 in).

Crocus chrysanthus *Flowering season* Late winter to mid-spring. *Uses* Full sun.

This species has typical crocus flowers, but they are only half the size of the much more widely planted large-flowered crocuses. It is especially useful for early flowers. There are many varieties, in shades and combinations of yellow, blue, and white. 8 cm (3 in).

Cyclamen hederifolium.

Crocus speciosus *Flowering season* Early to mid-autumn. *Uses* Full sun.

This is a rather fragile-looking crocus, but effective in a mass. The flowers are light mauve to purple, with yellow anthers and conspicuous orange-red stigmas. There are various named forms. 10 – 13 cm (4 – 5 in).

Crocus tommasinianus *Flowering season* Late winter to early spring. *Uses* Full sun.

The typical crocus flowers are normally clear mauve but other colours include reddish-mauve to warm purple. There are some named varieties. This crocus spreads easily. 8 cm (3 in).

Cyclamen hederifolium *Flowering season* Late summer to late autumn. *Uses* Leafy woodland soil; partial to full shade.

You may still find this listed as *C. neapolitanum*. It has ivy-shaped, marbled leaves, and mauve to pale pink miniature cyclamen flowers, although there is a white variety. It is easy to grow. 10 cm (4 in).

Cyclamen coum *Flowering season* Late winter to mid-spring. *Uses* Leafy woodland soil; partial to full shade.

The rounded or kidney-shaped leaves are dark red below, sometimes marbled on top. There are miniature cyclamen flowers in shades of pink or carmine, and also white. 8 cm (3 in).

Eranthis hyemalis (winter aconite) *Flowering season* Late winter to early

Eranthis hyemalis.

spring. *Uses* Leafy woodland soil; partial shade.

The vivid yellow flowers are set in a ruff of bright green leaves. This plant is sometimes difficult to establish from dry tubers, but easy once established. 10 cm (4 in).

Erythronium dens-canis (dog's tooth violet) *Flowering season* Mid-spring. *Uses* Leafy woodland soil; partial shade.

This plant has marbled or blotched foliage, and nodding flowers with usually pink or purple petals. It needs a damp, sheltered position, but will then naturalise well. 15 cm (6 in).

Fritillaria meleagris.

Galanthus sp. (snowdrops).

Fritillaria meleagris (snake's head fritillary) *Flowering season* Mid- to late spring. *Uses* Full sun or partial shade.

The nodding bell-shaped flowers are distinctively chequered. The colours range from creamy white through shades of rose and lilac to purple.

Galanthus nivalis (snowdrop) *Flowering season* Late winter to early spring. *Uses* Full sun or partial shade.

The snowdrop needs no description. There are many other species, and a number of varieties of the common snowdrop, but unless you want to form a collection of them *G. nivalis* is generally

cheaper and perfectly satisfactory for the rock garden. Ideally, they should be transplanted after flowering and before the leaves have died down, but you will have to order from a specialist to obtain plants 'in the green'. 10 – 15 cm (4 – 6 in).

Ipheion uniflorum *Flowering season* Mid- to late spring. *Uses* Full sun or partial shade.

This plant, also known as *Triteleia uniflora*, has dainty, star-shaped flowers. 'Wisley Blue' (mauve with orange stamens) is the form usually grown. It is best grown in a sheltered position. 13 cm (5 in).

Ipheion uniflorum.

Iris reticulata 'Pauline'.

Iris danfordiae *Flowering season* Late winter. *Uses* Full sun.

This species has deep lemon iris-type flowers with dark greenish-grey spots down the throat, and it is slightly fragrant. 10 cm (4 in) (leaves taller in summer).

Iris histrioides 'Major' *Flowering season* Late winter to early spring. *Uses* Full sun.

This one has deep blue iris flowers. The height given below is for the plant in bloom; the leaves grow considerably taller by the summer. 10 cm (4 in).

Iris reticulata *Flowering season* Early spring. *Uses* Full sun.

The flowers are up to 8 cm (3 in) across, in shades of blue or purple, with conspicuous orange ridges on the falls. There are several varieties. The leaves eventually add another 5 – 8 cm (2 – 3 in)

to the height stated below. 10 – 15 cm (4 – 6 in).

Muscari armeniacum (grape hyacinth) *Flowering season* Mid- to late spring. *Uses* Full sun or partial shade.

This plant has tightly-packed blue bells and stout stems. Each bulb usually produces several spikes. It is very easy to grow, multiplying freely. 15 – 20 cm (6 – 8 in).

Narcissus bulbocodium (hoop petticoat daffodil) *Flowering season* Early to mid-spring. *Uses* Full sun.

The vivid yellow funnel-shaped corona suggests a hooped petticoat. This plant is best in a moist position. 15 cm (6 in).

Narcissus canaliculatus *Flowering season* Mid-spring. *Uses* Full sun.

The flowers are formed in small clusters, and there is a reflexed white

Muscari armeniacum.

Narcissus cyclamineus.

perianth and small golden cups. It is fragrant. 15 cm (6 in).

Narcissus cyclamineus *Flowering season* Early spring. *Uses* Leafy woodland soil; full sun.

This plant has small clear yellow flowers with a much reflexed perianth. It is best in a moist position. There are several *N. cyclamineus* hybrids offered in catalogues. These are superb plants, but generally very different in appearance and not so well suited to the rock garden. 10 – 15 cm (4 – 6 in).

Narcissus triadrus albus (angel's tears) *Flowering season* Early to mid-spring. *Uses* Full sun.

The cluster of pendent flowers with globular cups and slightly reflexed perianth is creamy-white. 10 – 15 cm (4 – 6 in).

Ornithogalum balansae *Flowering season* Early to mid-spring. *Uses* Full sun or partial shade.

This plant has clusters of star-shaped white flowers striped green on the back. 10 cm (4 in).

Ornithogalum nutans *Flowering season* Mid-spring. *Uses* Leafy woodland soil; partial shade.

The spikes of green and white nodding bells are distinctive and attractive, but this plant needs a fairly good, humus-rich soil. 23 – 30 cm (9 – 12 in).

Puschkinia scilloides (striped squill) *Flowering season* Early spring. *Uses* Full sun or partial shade.

This species is also likely to be listed still as *P. libanotica*. These scilla-like plants have spikes of a dozen or more bell-like flowers, pale silver-blue with deep blue lines down the centre of the petals. There is also a white variety. 10 cm (4 in).

Rhodohypoxis baurii *Flowering season* Mid-spring to early autumn. *Uses* Acid soil; full sun; trough or sink.

The plant has corm-like rhizomes, and makes a tuft of pale green linear-lanceolate leaves. The rose-red flowers have petals arranged in two groups of three. There are forms varying from white to dark rose. Although it may succumb in a very severe winter, it is usually hardy. Protect for excessive moisture in winter. 8 cm (3 in).

Scilla sibirica *Flowering season* Early to mid-spring. *Uses* Full sun.

This is often spelt 'siberica'. It has slender stems of hanging, vivid blue flowers, and there are usually several flower stems from each bulb. 15 cm (6 in).

Sternbergia lutea (lily of the field) *Flowering season* Early to mid-autumn. *Uses* Full sun.

The flowers look like yellow crocuses. Although the leaves appear with the flowers they do not attain their full

Narcissus triandrus 'Albus'

Puschkinia libanotica.

Sternbergia lutea.

Scilla sibirica.

Tulipa tarda.

89

length until spring. They may take a couple of years to become established; do not disturb them. 15 cm (6 in).

Tulipa pulchella *Flowering season* Late winter to early spring. *Uses* Full sun.

The plant has narrow leaves, often margined red, and violet-red globe-shaped flowers, although there are varieties in other shades. 15 cm (6 in).

Tulipa tarda *Flowering season* Mid- to late spring. *Uses* Full sun.

This is a prolific tulip, each bulb often bearing five or six flowers that open flat to expose bright gold petals tipped white. 10 cm (4 in).

FERNS

The inclusion of ferns may seem a little surprising given that most hardy ferns like cool, moist conditions. Few of them will tolerate a normal rock garden, but in peat beds, and on the shady side of walls, they can be invaluable. Some ferns will, however, grow in rock crevices where they have to tolerate dry conditions. The hardy ferns listed here are only a small selection of those that might be suitable. They are not all widely sold in garden centres, but you can get them from a fern specialist, along with many more that would be suitable. All the ferns below are suitable for growing in crevices in a wall.

Asplenium ruta-muraria (wall rue) This is a particularly useful fern because it will grow in rock crevices and walls where it has to tolerate periods of drought. It is a tufted plant with stiff leaf stalks bearing irregularly fan-shaped thickish leaflets. It is a variable plant. 5 – 10 cm (2 – 4 in).

Asplenium trichomanes (maidenhair spleenwort) This adaptable fern is happy in crevices or even as a pot-plant. It makes a spreading clump with tufted habit. The thread-like black wiry stems bear many opposite pairs of small, almost round leaflets. It is best in alkaline soil, and is a plant for stone walls rather than a peat garden. 8 – 13 cm (3 – 5 in).

Phyllitis scolopendrium (hart's-tongue fern) Still sometimes sold as *Scolopendrium vulgare*, it may also be found as *Asplenium scolopendrium*. The evergreen leaves are entire and not

Phyllitis scolopendrium.

divided like most fern fronds. There are varieties with crinkly edges. 30 – 60 cm (1 – 2 ft).

Polypodium vulgare (polypody) The mid-green, drooping leathery fronds are deeply cut and resembling the teeth of a comb. This fern retains its colour until late into winter. There are several varieties, which will grow in sun or partial shade, and do well in stony ground. 15 – 30 cm (6 – 12 in).

DWARF SHRUBS

To exclude shrubs from a rock garden is to miss the chance to give it a backbone that will retain interest all the year round, but especially in winter when the shape and form, and sometimes colour, reduces the chances of it looking bleak.

The problem is one of size and scale.

Acer palmatum 'Dissectum Atropurpureum'.

All shrubs here will look perfectly in place in a rock garden of generous proportions; some of them could dominate a small rock outcrop or a very modest rock garden. In any rock garden there should be a place for *some* shrubs, but they will have to be chosen with care. Make a point of introducing at least a few shrubs, but place them carefully. Above all, make sure they really are dwarf: resist the temptation to buy shrubs that just *look* as though they will be dwarfs when you see them in the garden centre. If you do not know the habit of the plant, check before you buy and plant.

Some of the plants below are likely to be found among the shrubs at a garden centre, not with the alpines.

Acer palmatum (Japanese maple) *Foliage season* Mid-spring to early autumn. *Uses* Acid soil; partial shade.

Having stated the need for choosing only small shrubs it may seem odd to start the list with a potential tree; but the Japanese maples are very slow-growing and in their early years are very beautiful. If the rock garden is not a large one you may need to be prepared to remove it when it gets too large (so plant it where it will not cause chaos if that becomes necessary).

Grow varieties such as 'Atropurpureum' (red shoots, purple, lobed leaves), and 'Dissectum Atropurpureum' (similar colour but with finely fingered leaves). This plant needs a sheltered position. Cold spring winds or too much sun can burn the foliage.

Andromeda polifolia (bog rosemary) *Flowering season* Late spring to early summer. *Uses* Acid soil, partial shade.

This species has nodding pink bells on an evergreen bush. The variety 'Alba' is white. 30 cm (1 ft). *A.p.* 'Compacta' grows to 15 cm (6 in).

Berberis buxifolia 'Nana' *Flowering season* Early to mid-spring. *Foliage season* all year *Uses* Full sun or full shade.

This is a slow-growing compact evergreen berberis with box-like leaves. It seldom produces the small clusters of yellow flowers but is useful for providing a mound of green throughout the year. 45 cm (1½ ft).

Berberis thunbergii *Flowering season* Late spring. *Foliage season* Mid-spring to early autumn. *Uses* Full sun.

The species itself is totally unsuitable for a rock garden, but there are a few of its varieties that can be useful because they are dwarf and have coloured foliage. 'Atropurpurea Nana' has purple-red leaves and remains compact. Small pale yellow flowers and sometimes small scarlet berries are a bonus. 30–45 cm (1–1½ ft).

Calluna vulgaris (heather) *Flowering season* Mid-summer to late autumn. *Uses* Acid soil; full sun.

Although heathers are often grown in a bed of their own, or in association with conifers, they make good rock garden plants too. The flowering period and height will depend on the variety.

Calluna vulgaris 'Sunset'.

Ceratostigma plumbaginoides.

Varieties such as 'Gold Haze' and 'Robert Chapman' are worth growing for winter foliage colour alone. For a small rock garden choose the dwarfest kinds. 15–45 cm (6–18 in).

Cassiope lycopodioides *Flowering season* Mid- to late spring. *Uses* Acid soil; partial shade.

This is a prostrate shrub with slender wiry, much branched stems. It has dark green leaves and white bell-shaped flowers. It needs cool conditions. 5–8 cm (2–3 in).

Ceratostigma plumbaginoides *Flowering season* Mid- to late autumn. *Uses* Full sun; in wall.

Deep blue periwinkle-like flowers appear on leafy shoots. The foliage assumes attractive reddish tints in autumn. A spreading plant, the shoots root themselves; it is good as a ground cover, but otherwise may need trimming back. 25 cm (10 in).

Cornus canadensis *Flowering season* Early summer. *Uses* Acid soil; partial shade.

This plant is best as a carpeter for moist woodland, but it is also a useful plant for a peat garden or a position in the rock garden that is not too dry. The greenish-purple true flowers are inconspicuous among the four bold white bracts that encircle them. 15–20 cm (6–8 in).

Cotoneaster dammeri *Flowering season* Early summer. *Uses* Full sun; ground cover.

This is a prostrate, evergreen ground-

Cytisus × kewensis

hugging shrub. It will spread to about 1.8 m (6 ft) with time, so it is only suitable for a large rock garden. The white flowers are insignificant, but the sealing-wax-red berries in autumn are very decorative.

Cytisus × beanii *Flowering season* Late spring. *Uses* Full sun.

This plant is a spectacular sight in bloom, when it is covered with masses of golden-yellow pea-type flowers. It spreads to about 90 cm (3 ft). 45–60 cm (1½–2 ft).

C. × kewensis *Flowering season* Late spring. *Uses* Full sun.

This is a procumbent plant with a spread of up to 1.2 m (4 ft), so it is only suitable for a large rock garden. It produces a profusion of pale yellow flowers. 30–60 cm (1–2 ft).

Daphne cneorum (garland flower) *Flowering season* Late spring to early summer. *Uses* Leafy woodland soil; full sun or partial shade.

This procumbent evergreen shrub spreading to about 60–90 cm (2–3 ft) produces dense terminal clusters of

Daphne cneorum 'Variegatum'.

fragrant rose-pink flowers. 'Eximia' is perhaps the finest form. There is also a white-flowered variety. 15 cm (6 in).

Erica herbacea (heath, heather)
Flowering season Late autumn to late spring. *Uses* Full sun.

Often still listed as *E. carnea*, this heather is too well known to need description, and is invaluable for winter colour. Flowering time and height will

Erica carnea 'Aurea'.

depend on the variety. Choose low, compact varieties for a small rock garden. Although ericas will usually grow in alkaline soils, they do not normally do well on *shallow* chalk soils. 15 – 30 cm (6 – 12 in).

Fuchsia 'Tom Thumb' *Flowering season* Early summer to early autumn. *Uses* Full sun.

Fuchsias may seem strange bedfellows for true alpines, but this variety is a charming dwarf plant if you can find a suitable setting for it. Red sepals, mauve petals. 30 cm (1 ft).

Gaultheria procumbens (creeping wintergreen) *Flowering season* Mid-to-late summer. *Uses* Acid soil; partial or full shade.

This makes a dense evergreen carpet of foliage, spreading to about 90 cm (3 ft). The pinkish-white urn-shaped flowers are followed by long-lasting bright red berries that nestle among the leaves. 10 – 15 cm (4 – 6 in).

Genista lydia *Flowering season* Early summer. *Uses* Full sun; in wall.

Fuchsia 'Tom Thumb'.

Genista lydia.

The slender arching branches smothered with yellow flowers are a spectacular sight, but with a spread of up to 1.8 m (6 ft) it is a plant for only the largest rock gardens. 60–90 cm (2–3 ft).

Genista pilosa 'Procumbens' *Flowering season* Late spring to mid-summer. *Uses* Full sun; in wall.

This prostrate shrub with a tangled mass of whip-like shoots spreads up to 90 cm (3 ft). It has a profusion of small yellow flowers. 8 cm (3 in).

Hebe 'Carl Teschner' *Flowering season* Early to mid-summer. *Uses* Full sun.

This hummock-forming spreading shrub with dense evergreen growth has grey-green leaves and violet-blue flower spikes. It is fairly hardy. 25–30 cm (10–12 in).

Hebe loganioides *Flowering season* Early to mid-summer. *Uses* Full sun.

This slow-growing shrublet with golden foliage has white flowers. 15 cm (6 in).

Hebe pinguifolia 'Pagei' *Flowering season* Late spring. *Foliage season* All year. *Uses* Full sun.

This may be listed simply as H. 'Pagei'. It has grey evergreen foliage, with the bonus of white flowers in spring. It forms a spreading clump. 15–23 cm (6–9 in).

Helianthemum.

Helianthemum nummularium (rock rose) *Flowering season* Early to mid-summer. *Uses* Full sun; in wall.

The species has yellow flowers but it is the many varieties of it that are grown, and these include shades of yellow, orange, pink and red. Some are double. All make excellent rock garden plants. 10 – 15 cm (4 – 6 in).

Hypericum olympicum *Flowering season* Mid- to late summer. *Uses* Full sun; trough or sink.

This plant has masses of slender upright stems and large golden flowers up to 5 cm (2 in) across. 23 cm (9 in).

Hypericum polyphyllum *Flowering season* Mid-summer to early autumn. *Uses* Full sun.

The leafy shoots are covered with yellow flowers, usually flushed red in bud, in summer. 'Sulphureum' has pale yellow flowers. 15 cm (6 in).

Hypericum polyphyllum citrinum.

Iberis gibraltarica *Flowering season* Mid- to late spring. *Uses* Full sun.

This evergreen sub-shrub has flattened heads of white, pink or lilac flowers. Although of doubtful hardiness in cold areas, it is easily propagated from seed. It needs a warm position. 30 cm (1 ft).

Iberis sempervirens (perennial candytuft) *Flowering season* Late spring to early summer. *Uses* Full sun; in wall.

This spreading, bushy evergreen has flat heads of white flowers. 'Snowflake' is a popular variety, but 'Little Gem' is about 10 cm (4 in) shorter. 25 cm (10 in).

Lithospermum diffusum 'Heavenly Blue' *Flowering season* Early summer to mid-autumn. *Uses* Full sun; ground cover.

This variety has spreading prostrate stems, and deep blue flowers 12 mm (½ in) across. It is useful ground cover in the rock garden. 8 – 10 cm (3 – 4 in).

Iberis sempervirens.

Rhododendron *Flowering season* Spring to early summer. *Uses* Acid soil; full sun or partial shade.

If you do not have a peaty or acid soil there is little point in struggling to grow rhododendrons in the rock garden; after all they flower in spring and early summer when there is competition from plenty of other plants. If you do have an acid soil, or have a peat bed, then you will almost certainly want to grow more rhododendrons than there is space to mention in a short entry. Avoid the large-flowered hybrids, which are generally out of keeping with a rock garden, and keep to the dwarf species, or low-growing hybrids such as 'Blue Tit'.

ROCK GARDEN CONIFERS

Not everyone likes conifers in a rock garden, but they almost always add interest at times when the other alpines

Abies balsamea 'Hudsonia'.

are not at their best. Used creatively, they help to provide a backbone shape along with the rocks. This is most obvious in winter, when the rocks and dwarf conifers can be seen in a light not so obvious in spring and summer.

The problem is integration. Too many small columnar conifers are likely to have the same effect as too many upright labels; they detract more than enhance. A mixture of shapes, including some that have a prostrate or hummock-forming habit, will do much to overcome this risk.

The 14 conifers below are among the most useful for alpine gardeners, but there are very many more candidates from which to choose if you consult a specialist conifer catalogue. Beware of descriptions, however, as some plants described as 'dwarf' conifers will quite soon outgrow a typical rock garden.

Most of the conifers below prefer a moist but well-drained position. The junipers are very drought-resistant.

Chamaecyparis lawsoniana 'Minima Aurea'.   *Chamaecyparis obtusa* 'Nana Gracilis'.

Abies balsamea 'Hudsonia' *Uses* Full
sun; trough or sink.

This conifer is slow-growing and a
compact, rounded shape, with dark green
aromatic foliage. It will tolerate chalky
soil well.

Chamaecyparis lawsoniana 'Minima
Aurea' *Uses* Full sun.

The tightly-packed yellow foliage
makes a rounded pyramid. It is especially
attractive in winter, but a very slow
grower.

Juniperus communis 'Depressa Aurea'.

Chamaecyparis lawsoniana 'Minima Glauca' *Uses* Full sun.

This forms a globular bush with dense sprays of sea green foliage.

Chamaecyparis obtusa 'Nana Aurea' *Uses* Full sun.

This slow-growing conical bush has yellow foliage that turns bronze in winter.

C. obtusa 'Nana Gracilis' *Uses* Full sun.

This is a slow-growing conical bush with shell-shaped sprays of dark green foliage.

C. obtusa 'Pygmaea' *Uses* Full sun.

This conifer has a semi-prostrate habit, and flattish fan-shaped branches with bright green leaves, turning bronze in winter.

Chamaecyparis pisifera 'Filifera Nana Aurea' *Uses* Full sun.

This low mop-headed bush, wider than it is high and with a conical top, has golden thread-like foliage.

Juniperus communis 'Compressa' *Uses* Full sun; trough or sink.

A miniature columnar tree, this variety has closely-packed grey-green foliage. It is one of the best rock-garden conifers.

J. communis 'Depressa Aurea' *Uses* Full sun.

This wide-spreading semi-prostrate bush, which is golden in summer (especi-

ally bright as the new shoots grow) and bronze in winter, needs to be in full sun.

Juniperus sabina 'Tamariscifolia' *Uses* Full sun.

This juniper is prostrate, but wide-spreading with age, reaching up to 3 m (10 ft) across; so it is only suitable for a very large rock garden unless you are willing to keep it pruned back.

Picea abies 'Nidiformis' *Uses* Full sun; trough or sink.

On this flat-topped bush with a spreading habit, the horizontal branches are arranged in tiers. The top of the plant often has a hollow appearance.

Thuja orientalis 'Rosedalis' *Uses* Full sun.

This is an interesting conifer that changes colour with the seasons. New

Picea abies 'Nidiformis'.

Thuja orientalis 'Aurea Nana'.

Asperula azurea (A. orientalis) 'Setosa'.

growth starts creamy yellow in spring, becomes pale green in summer, and turns purplish in winter. It is oval in outline and needs a sheltered position.

Thuja orientalis 'Aurea Nana' The oval outline is formed of crowded upright branches. It is golden yellow in summer, becoming bronzed in winter.

Tsuga canadensis 'Cole' With a prostrate habit and very slow growth, this conifer is for creeping over rocks. It often has a nest-like depression of bare branches in the centre.

ANNUALS IN THE ROCK GARDEN

Hardy annuals are one solution to the need for quick colour and interest in a newly-constructed rock garden. They also have a role to play in an established rock garden, bringing pockets of colour when the main flush of spring flowers is over.

They should be introduced with thought, however, as by their very nature they must seed freely and germinate easily, as this is their only method of perpetuation. That can mean lots of self-sown seedlings to be thinned or weeded out in subsequent years.

The following is a selection of hardy annuals that look good in a rock garden. Most of them are widely available, but a few are supplied by just a few seedsmen, so you may have to check a few catalogues for them.

Adonis aestivalis (pheasant's eye) This plant has feathery foliage and cup-shaped crimson flowers with dark centres. 30 cm (1 ft).

Ionopsidium acaule.

Alyssum, sweet The popular edging alyssum needs no introduction. There are pink and purple varieties but white is still the most popular. Choose a compact variety such as 'Snow Carpet'; some varieties are too straggly. It is a good plant to grow between paving.

Asperula azurea 'Setosa' This may be listed as *Asperula orientalis*. It has fluffy-looking heads of pale blue fragrant flowers and can be straggly, and out of place in a small rock garden. 30 cm (1 ft).

Ionopsidium acaule (violet cress) This is one of the most suitable hardy annuals for the rock garden, and it is also useful between paving, producing low mounds of pale mauve flowers. 5 cm (2 in).

Kaulfussia amelloides This plant has small bright blue daisy-like flowers, and needs a sunny position. It is also suitable for dry walls. 15 cm (6 in).

Kaulfussia amelloides.

Leptosiphon hybridus.

106

Limnanthes douglasii.

Leptosiphon, mixed hybrids (stardust) With masses of star-shaped flowers in shades of cream, yellow, pink, orange, and red, this annual needs to be grown in a mass for effect. 8 cm (3 in).

Limnanthes douglasii (poached egg flower) This species has bright green ferny foliage, saucer-shaped yellow flowers tipped white, and a spreading habit. 15 cm (6 in).

Linaria 'Fairy Bouquet'.

Nemophila menziesii (N. insignis).

Linaria maroccana (toadflax) The flowers are rather like miniature snap-dragons (antirrhinums) in many colours, including pinks, reds, yellows, and white. If you trim off the dead flowers once they have finished, there is often a second flush of flowers later in the season. 23–30 cm (9–12 in).

Nemophila insignis (baby blue eyes) With feathery foliage, and sky-blue cup-shaped flowers with white centres, this carpeting annual is better in a moist, cool position than a hot, dry spot in the rock garden. 15 cm (6 in).

Phacelia campanularia This annual has gentian-blue flowers with white centres, like upturned bells. 23 cm (9 in).

8·BUYING AND PLANTING

Nowadays garden centres have an enormous range of alpines (they are just as likely to be labelled 'rock plants'), including some that are quite uncommon, even obscure. The range is likely to vary widely from one garden centre to the next, which can make it difficult to obtain a particular plant without a lot of visits or phone calls, but it can make shopping for alpines an interesting or exciting experience.

At the end of this chapter there are some suggested starter collections if you found the list of plants in Chapter 7 just too bewildering. These have been kept to fairly widely available plants that you should not have much difficulty in obtaining, except for the tufa selection for which you will probably have to go to a specialist supplier. One of the best ways of choosing your rock plants is to make a note of those growing in other people's gardens that you like. This will give you a much better idea of what the plants are like than any catalogue or book. Rock gardens in public and botanic gardens can be particularly useful because they are usually labelled. Be more cautious about deciding on a plant that you see exhibited at a show. These plants can sometimes look very different as a mature plant in the garden.

To be more certain of obtaining some of the less common alpines you will probably have to go to a specialist alpine nursery. Visit it personally if you can because it will be an interesting experience and the plants are less likely to suffer in transit. For many people, however, this simply is not feasible, and all the major alpine specialists offer a mail-order service. You will find the addresses of many of them in gardening magazines, but if you are going into alpine gardening in an enthusiastic way it is best to join a club. Their newsletters or bulletins will almost certainly contain the names of many specialist nurseries. You must expect to pay a bit more when buying the plants in this way, not only because they are likely to be the less common sorts that you order but also because the carriage charge is likely to be significant on a small order.

Plants get you off to a good start, and are really the only practical method if you are planting a rock garden from scratch, as you hardly want to wait several years for results from seed.

Once the basic planting is established, however, seed is a serious contender. It will sometimes enable you to obtain a large number of plants relatively cheaply, and give you the possibility of growing many plants that you are unlikely to find in nurseries, especially if you take part in the seed distribution of specialist societies.

Tips on raising your own plants from seed are given in Chapter 10.

HOW TO ASSESS QUALITY

If you are buying by mail-order there is nothing much you can do about poor plants, apart from complain. At a garden centre you can leave them there if they are not up to scratch. If there are several plants to choose from it is useful to know what you should be looking for.

Do not buy plants with brown, dead or withered leaves, unless it is the end of winter and these are the normal results of the winter period. Avoid plants with

It pays to choose your plants carefully. Quality is inevitably variable. These two specimens of *Thymus vulgaris* 'Golden King' were bought from the same garden centre on the same day. They cost the same. The one on the left was old starved stock that had been neglected, the one on the right a healthy and vigorous plant that had been received from the grower more recently.

excessively lush or lanky growth; compact plants (for the type) and symmetrical growth are good signs.

The leaves should have good colour. Avoid any with yellowish leaves, unless it is clearly a plant that is supposed to have golden foliage. Weedy growth in the pot can be a sign of neglect, apart from which you do not want to introduce weeds into the rock garden.

WHEN TO PLANT

Practically all rock garden plants (other than bulbs, corms and tubers) are sold growing in pots, so there is no problem about planting them at almost any time. However, it is probably not a good idea to plant after early autumn, and spring is a particularly good time (even though some of them may be coming into flower). Late summer is another good time.

There is no mystery about planting alpines (planting in tufa calls for a special technique but this is described on page 46).

Always water the pot about an hour before planting. If there is any weed growth in the pot, carefully remove the top 6 – 12 mm (¼ – ½ in) of compost.

Make the planting hole about 8 cm (3 in) wider than the diameter of the rootball, and if the planting soil is very dry, fill up the hole with water, with the plant in position, before firming the soil around the plant. Keep the plants well watered during the first summer.

In small areas, and in troughs, single

To ensure that the soil around the roots is free-draining, add a handful of grit.

plants of one kind will be satisfactory. In the larger rock garden plant in bolder groups of three or more plants if possible. This does not apply so much to dwarf shrubs and conifers, but certainly to most alpines.

It is a good idea to label the plants. Some people simply dislike their rock garden being cluttered with labels, but you will probably forget exactly what most of the unlabelled plants are within a year or two.

If you do decide to use labels, there is the ever-present problem of them becoming illegible if not lost. Lead or aluminium labels are generally the least

Knock the plant out of the pot, disturbing the roots as little as possible.

Firm the plant well, ensuring there are no air pockets, which may cause the roots to dry out.

obtrusive, and they will be permanent by label standards if you can stamp the name on with a die.

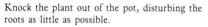

A BEGINNER'S COLLECTION FOR A TROUGH

Achillea 'King Edward'
Aethionema 'Warley Rose'
Arabis ferdinandi-coburgi 'Variegata'
Aster alpinus
Campanula carpatica
Dianthus (small kinds such as 'Little Jock')
Gentiana acaulis

Hypericum olympicum
Phlox douglasii
Potentilla tabernaemontani
Raoulia australis
Rhodohypoxis baurii
Saxifraga aizoon
Sedum lydium
Sempervivum tectorum

A COLLECTION FOR A TUFA DISPLAY

Many of these will have to be acquired from an alpine specialist.
Androsace sempervivoides

Arenaria tetraquetra
Armeria caespitosa
Asperula nitida
Asplenium trichomanes
Daphne alpina
Dianthus haematocalyx
Draba aizoides
Draba bryoides imbricata
Edraianthus pumilio
Myosotis rupricola
Phlox douglasii
Primula allionii
Saxifraga aizoon 'Minutifolia'
Saxifraga aretioides
Saxifraga burserana
Saxifraga caesia
Saxifraga cochlearis 'Minor'
Saxifraga 'Jenkinsae'
Saxifraga squarrosa
Sempervivum allionii
Sempervivum arachnoideum

20 USEFUL WALL PLANTS

Acaena microphylla (top or face)
Achillea tomentosa (top)
Alyssum montanum (top)
Alyssum saxatile (top or face)
Arabis caucasica (top or face)
Arenaria balaerica (top or face)
Aubrieta (face)
Campanula garganica (face)
Cerastium tomentosum (face)
Corydalis lutea (face)
Dianthus deltoides (top or face)
Erinus alpinus (top or face)
Gypsophila repens (top or face)
Iberis sempervirens (top or face)

Phyllitis scolopendrium (face)
Polypodium vulgare (face)
Saponaria ocymoides (top or face)
Sedum (many) (face)
Sempervivum tectorum (and many others)
(top or face)
Silene schafta (top)

A STARTER COLLECTION FOR A ROCK GARDEN

Acaena microphylla
Alyssum saxatile
Anayclus depressus
Antennaria dioica 'Rosea'
Arabis ferdinandi-coburgi 'Variegata'
Armeria maritima
Aubrieta
Campanula carpatica
Campanula cochleariifolia
Campanula garganica
Cotyledon simplicifolia
Dianthus deltoides
Dryas octopetala
Erinus alpinus
Gentiana acaulis
Gentiana septemfida
Gentiana sino-ornata
Geranium sanguineum 'Lancastriense'
Geranium subcaulescens
Gypsophila repens
Hebe 'Carl Teschner'
Hebe pinguifolia 'Pagei'
Helianthemum
Hypericum olympicum
Iberis sempervirens 'Snowflake'
Lithospermum diffusum 'Heavenly Blue'
Mazus reptans

Oxalis adenophylla
Phlox douglasii
Phlox subulata
Primula auricula
Pulsatilla vulgaris
Raoulia australis
Saxifraga aizoon (various varieties)
Saxifraga (mossy type)
Sedum floriferum 'Weihenstephaner Gold'

Sedum spathulifolium 'Capablanca'
Sedum spathulifolium 'Purpureum'
Sempervivum (various)
Silene schafta
Thymus × citriodorus 'Aureus'
Thymus serpyllum (various varieties)
Veronica prostrata

9·ROUTINE CARE

No part of the garden stands still, and gradual deterioration will set in unless you do something to stem it. This applies as much to the rock garden as anywhere else, and though most alpines are tough many will succumb to competition from weeds and perhaps even from each other if vigorous and more restrained plants are put in close proximity. Routine care will often prevent the need for more drastic action later, so it is worth working to a plan.

WEEDING

Weeding is one of the most important jobs, and often the one most delayed. The weed problem will be much reduced by a suitable stone mulch (see below).

Herbicides (weedkillers) can play an important role in clearing the ground before building a rock garden, but with a few exceptions are of little use for broad-leaved weeds in an established rock garden.

The exceptions are, however, important ones. Alloxydim sodium can be used to kill grass among broad-leaved rock plants. You will need to follow the manufacturer's instructions carefully, but applied at the right time in the right way

this can control grasses that were once an intractable problem in a rock garden.

Glyphosate is a systemic insecticide that will kill your alpines as readily as the weeds, but you can paint it on to the leaves of difficult weeds that may have established a perennial root system beneath the rocks. It will be translocated from the leaves to kill the roots too. So for a particularly difficult perennial weed it may be worth taking a little trouble to treat it in this way. Again, you need to follow the instructions very carefully.

For annual weeds, and the many self-sown seedlings, there is no easy alternative to hand weeding. It is best to look on this in a positive way and regard it as a way of getting to know your plants well at close quarters.

The worst annual weeds are those that grow, flower and seed in a very short time, and even seem to keep on growing through the winter. Such weeds should be pursued ruthlessly, for once missed and allowed to go unchecked they will soon become a major problem that is difficult to eradicate. A plant sometimes deliberately *introduced* into the rock garden can be an equal menace: one such example is *Sedum acre*.

A concentrated effort on weeds during the first two seasons will do much to minimise the problem for future years, although it will still be a job that needs regular attention.

Stone chipping mulches will reduce the problem of weeds as well as keeping the alpines clear of wet soil. Grit and pea gravel can be equally effective. Whatever material is used it inevitably begins to get mixed in with the underlying soil in time. Each winter, go round the rock garden and top up the chippings or gravel wherever necessary.

PRUNING AND TRIMMING

Pruning and trimming may be another way of saying 'hack back'. Certainly vigorous plants such as aubrieta and *Alyssum saxatile* are best cut back with shears after flowering, both to improve appearance and to keep the plants compact; but any plant of a spreading nature that is outgrowing its allotted space will need cutting back annually, otherwise less vigorous plants may be overrun. You can afford to be ruthless with aggressive plants, because they will almost certainly bounce back. The best time to do this is after flowering.

Shrubby plants may need annual pruning (heathers benefit from having the flower stems clipped back after flowering for instance); others may simply need dead or diseased wood cutting out. Generally, however, little pruning other than dead-heading is required on the rock garden.

Dress the surface with shingle or stone chippings to improve appearance, keep water from the neck of the plants, and to some extent deter slugs and snails.

If slugs are a problem, it is worth using slug pellets to control them.

REPLACING AND REPLANTING

This is not something that you need to worry about for a few years, but it has been estimated that the average life of an alpine in the wild is about seven years. In the garden many will begin to deteriorate after four or five years. This means that after several years there is a need for constant replenishment. Regular propagation will ensure that this should cost you little, but you need to have new plants coming along as replacements *before* the old ones die. Sometimes self-sown seedlings will solve the problem for you.

Correcting errors is an inevitable task in the early years. Quite simply plants do not always perform as we expect and whether it is because the plant simply is not suited (or too well suited and has become rather rampant), or whether it was a lack of understanding and research beforehand, some fail and others overtake. Sometimes plants that are perfectly acceptable on their own just do not go well together. There is no point in accepting this as inevitable; be prepared to move or replace a plant if necessary.

FEEDING

Feeding is often neglected; after all, mountain plants are usually growing on poor soil. Nevertheless, feeding without encouraging lush growth will delay the day when a much more drastic soil change or improvement becomes necessary.

Dusting with bonemeal once a year may be all that is necessary, although a little sulphate of potash too will probably improve things. General fertilisers should not be necessary, and you should certainly avoid applying nitrogenous fertilisers on their own.

It is a good idea to apply a top dressing of peat and grit in the autumn, and a little bonemeal can be mixed in with this. It will probably be the only feeding necessary.

10·PROPAGATION

To start with it makes sense to buy most of your plants; you will save at least a season, probably many more. Once the basic planting is complete it makes sense to propagate your own plants, in order to provide replacements as existing plants deteriorate or die, and to broaden both the range of plants and the hobby.

The suggested methods of propagation in Chapter 7 are generally the easiest or most straightforward, but there are often other options too if you want to experiment.

The basic methods of propagation are illustrated and described below, but do not overlook the role of hardy annuals,

Some seeds have a dormancy that is difficult to break without a period of chilling. These are mixed gentian seeds about to be chilled in a fridge for several weeks (see text).

which you can sow where they are to flower. These can be especially useful while the rock garden is becoming established, but be warned that some of them seed freely and you could have a problem with self-sown seedlings in future years.

For some plants you have the option of seed or a vegetative method such as cuttings. Bear in mind that although seed should produce plants true to type for the species, hybrids and varieties are likely to produce variable plants, and for these vegetative propagation is a surer way of getting the plants that you want.

GROWING FROM SEED

Seed is an important method of propagation for alpines. Many new species have been introduced into cultivation from seed, and it is also widely used for commercial propagation.

Unfortunately alpines as a group are very variable and sometimes demanding in their requirements. Most of them need a period of chilling before they germinate; others need to be sown as soon as possible after ripening. The step-by-step instructions below apply to most of the plants for which seed has been suggested in Chapter 7. If seed is an especially diffi-cult method it has not been suggested, and variations to the advice below have been noted.

As a general rule for any plant for which you have seed but no instructions, sow a pinch as soon as possible after ripening or as soon as you receive the seeds, and the rest in late winter. The chances are you should get results from one of the sowings. Some seeds can take years to germinate, however, so do not throw the seed pans or pots out too quickly.

Many alpines germinate only after a period of dormancy, which is usually broken by a period of exposure to low temperatures. For that reason it is often a good idea to sow in late autumn or early winter and leave them in a cold frame for the winter (the compost should be moist). Nothing will happen until spring, but simply sowing in spring without the exposure to cold may result in poor germination (or a year's delay).

You can speed the process up by pre-chilling the seeds, putting them between layers of damp kitchen paper in a covered container in the fridge. The paper must be kept moist (but not waterlogged). After about four weeks the seeds can be sown normally. This is a useful method if you receive the seed too late to sow and leave outdoors for the winter, or if you simply did not get round to it.

How to sow

1) You are unlikely to need a large quantity of plants so sow thinly in pots or seed pans. Crock the bottom of the pot

Most alpines are best sown in pots. Firm the compost first with a flat surface.

Distribute the seeds as evenly as possible over the surface.

with old broken pots, or better still a perforated zinc disc (this will prevent worms getting into the pot). Plastic pots are suitable for seed-sowing.

2) A mixture of two parts loam-based seed compost to one part of sharp sand will be suitable for most seeds, although an ericaceous loam-based compost and sand should be used for lime-hating plants. Fill it to within 12 mm (½ in) of the rim, then level and firm the surface. Stand the pot in a dish of water until the compost is damp. When the surface darkens, remove the pot and let it drain.

3) Sow thinly. Very fine seeds should be sown on the surface; large seeds should be covered with their own depth of compost unless you know that the seed has other requirements. Finish off by sprinkling just enough very fine stone chippings, gravel, or grit (no more than 3 mm or ⅛ in) to cover the surface. You can buy grit used for poultry. This treatment discourages the growth of algae and mosses, which can be a problem with pots that may have to stand for a year or more before germination.

4) Cover the pot with a small sheet of glass to conserve moisture, and if water is needed try to supply it from below. Plunging the pot to the rim in a bed of grit or damp peat will do much to keep the compost moist, and if the plunge material is kept moist the pots may receive enough moisture by capillary action. If you find the chore of watering the pots by immersion just too tedious, use a very fine mist of water from a compression sprayer, or a fine-rosed watering-can.

Cover the surface with a thin layer of coarse grit, and do not forget to label.

Water the pot by standing it in a bowl of water, so that the seeds do not get washed away.

5) Thin early, using tweezers to remove any that are very close together. Leave the other seedlings to grow on a little longer.

6) Prick out into pots (vigorous, fast-growing plants like aubrieta and cerastium can be pricked out into seed trays). Most should be pricked out when they have produced three or four small leaves, although bulb seedlings are left in the original pots for the first season.

Some alpine seedlings are small and difficult to handle and you will have to wait until they are large enough to handle before pricking them out into small pots. Always hold them by a leaf and not the stem.

CUTTINGS

Most alpines can be propagated from cuttings, and this often saves a year to get a plant of equal size. There is also the advantage that varieties and hybrids that might not come true from seed will be exactly like the parent. Within reason, the smaller the cutting the more likely it is to root. There are many ideas of what a good cuttings compost should be, and most of them are successful. Equal parts fine peat and coarse sand, or 2 parts peat to 1 part sand, work well. Other gardeners prefer vermiculite or perlite on their own or as an added ingredient.

When to take cuttings No one time is

Prepare a cutting by stripping off the lower leaves (left).

ideal for all plants. Most spring-flowering alpines produce new growth after flowering, and these make good cuttings in early or mid-summer. Do not worry if they are small; 1.5 – 4 cm (½ – 1½ in) is about right for most.

Cuttings of more mature wood can be taken in late summer and early autumn, and these are likely to be a bit larger.

Dip the end into a rooting hormone (below).

To provide a humid atmosphere, put the pot in a polythene bag and tie the top. Use a few small canes to keep the bag off the cuttings. Fungus diseases are often a problem in a closed humid atmosphere like this, so it pays to spray the cuttings with a fungicide first.

Insert the cuttings around the edge of the pot.

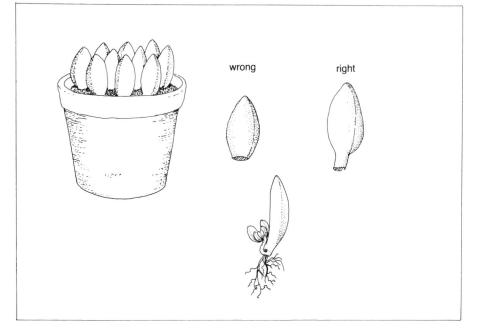

wrong

right

Some alpines with succulent leaves, many sedums for example, can be propagated from leaf cuttings. Remove the complete leaf carefully, and leave it exposed for a day or two before inserting in the compost.

How to take cuttings

1) Using a non-flowering shoot, cut through the stem just below a leaf joint with a sharp knife. If you are dealing with a plant that has a hollow or pithy stem, detach a small branch together with a heel (sliver of the main branch). Trim the base of the heel neatly with a sharp knife.

2) Dip the cutting into a rooting hormone, then insert the cuttings in a cutting compost, firming it round the shoots.

3) Water, preferably with a fungicide added, then place in a propagator, closed frame, or enclosed with a polythene (polyethylene) bag. If not in an enclosed environment like a bag, mist regularly. Keep shaded, and never let the compost dry out.

4) Once the cuttings have rooted, pot them up using a proper potting compost (there are practically no nutrients in the cutting mixtures mentioned earlier).

Leaf cuttings Some rock plants, such as ramondas and some sedums and crassulas, can be propagated from leaves. The ramondas have to be taken with a leaf stalk removed with a firm downward pull to secure the portion of the leaf that

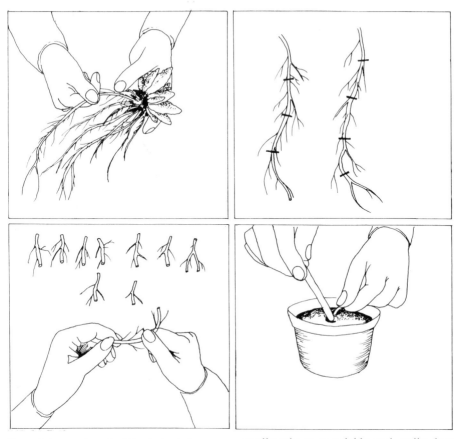

Some alpines, such as the *Primula denticulata* illustrated here, can be raised from root cuttings. Each root can be cut into several sections, but make sure you remember which is the top of each piece!

clasps the central stem. They should be taken in early or mid-summer and inserted in the compost for one-third of their length. The easiest leaf cuttings are the stalkless type such as sedums and crassulas. Simply push the stem end of each leaf into a gritty compost. They will usually take root quickly and easily, but do not overwater.

Root cuttings are used for a few plants which are not easy to propagate in other ways. Cut the fleshy roots into 2.5 cm (1 in) lengths and insert in a cuttings compost with the top just level with the surface. To avoid confusion between top and bottom, make a straight cut across the top and a sloping cut at the bottom as you make the cuttings.

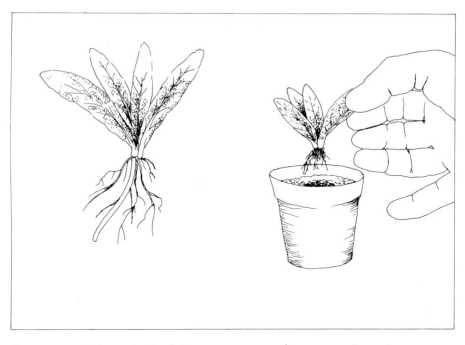

Once a root cutting has produced sufficient leaves, pot it up as a young plant.

DIVISION

Plants with an extensive fibrous root system can usually be divided (although for those plants that resent root disturbance it is not a good idea). Some clump-forming plants are simple to divide into individual shoots with a root system once the plant has been lifted; but those with a creeping rootstock such as many primulas may have to be cut with a knife. Some plants that form a fibrous-rooted clump are best divided by lifting and forcing portions apart with two hand-forks inserted back-to-back and levered against each other.

When to divide Most plants are best divided after flowering or in early autumn. Divisions made in summer must be kept well watered, and preferably shaded, until re-established.